Catalogue of the Manx crosses with the runic inscriptions and various readings and renderings compared

Kermode, Philip Moore Callow, 1854 or 5-1932

CATALOGUE

OF

MANKS CROSSES.

CATALOGUE

OF THE

MANKS CROSSES

WITH THE

RUNIC INSCRIPTIONS

AND VARIOUS

READINGS AND RENDERINGS

COMPARED.

BY

P. M. C. KERMODE, F.S.A. Scot.

Second Edition.

ISLE OF MAN:
C. B. HEYES, *RAMSEY COURIER* OFFICE
LONDON:
WILLIAMS & NORGATE, 14, Henrietta Street, Covent Garden.
EDINBURGH:
WILLIAMS & NORGATE, 20, South Frederick Street.

Mulhern

TO

GEORGE STEPHENS, F.S.A.,

HON. DOCTOR OF LETTERS, CAMBRIDGE,

ENGLAND,

PROFESSOR OF OLD ENGLISH AND OF THE ENGLISH LANGUAGE

IN THE

UNIVERSITY OF COPENHAGEN,

ETC., ETC.,

𝔗𝔥𝔦𝔰 𝔏𝔦𝔱𝔱𝔩𝔢 𝔙𝔬𝔩𝔲𝔪𝔢 𝔦𝔰 𝔇𝔢𝔡𝔦𝔠𝔞𝔱𝔢𝔡,

AS A

SLIGHT TRIBUTE OF RESPECT AND ADMIRATION FOR

HIS GREAT WORK

ON

"THE OLD NORTHERN RUNIC MONUMENTS OF SCANDINAVIA

AND ENGLAND."

Preface to Second Edition.

SINCE this little Catalogue was first published, more of our ancient Crosses have been brought to light, short descriptions of which are here included. The Author gladly avails himself also of the opportunity to correct several errors which, unfortunately, crept into the First Edition, in consequence of its having been put through the press very hurriedly. Besides this the Ogham Inscriptions are now added.

An alteration is made in the arrangement, some, which in the First Edition were added separately as being of rather different character and of earlier date, being here included and numbered with the rest. The descriptions have been all carefully revised, and some of them entirely re-written. By the kind courtesy of the Society of Antiquaries of Scotland, three most interesting Crosses figured in their Proceedings,* from photographs by Mr G. Patterson, are here reproduced.

The larger work referred to in the Introduction is still in hand —the expense of illustrations, such as the Author wishes to have, being more than at present he can undertake. He hopes,

---

* NOTE.—Proceedings of the Society of Antiquaries of Scotland, 1886-87, p.p. 328 and 331; and 1888-89, p.p. 333, 336, 337 and 338, where they form illustrations to valuable papers on these Crosses by Mr George F. Black,

however, to be able before long to publish a limited number of copies for subscribers. One advantage of the delay will be that some Crosses not before known will now be figured and described. The Author has himself had the good fortune to have been instrumental in bringing to light a dozen Crosses or their remains, some from walls into which they had been built, one from a flight of steps, one from a pig-stye. There are at least three others which he would like to have taken out to be figured, namely, two at Maughold, one a lintel over the door-way and one over the east window, and one in the Cathedral wall at Peel.

As regards the reference to profits (First Edition, Introduction p. 7) those who have had a wider experience than the Author in such matters will not be surprised to hear that there were none,—in fact he was out of pocket by the transaction. He feels greatly encouraged, however, by the very friendly and sympathetic way in which his Catalogue was reviewed, both by Newspapers and Scientific Journals, at home and abroad, and is gratified to think that it has been of some service in spreading the knowledge of these most valuable and interesting remains and the desire for their preservation.

In the meantime he is having made a complete set of Casts, only a few having been previously taken, of which some are much damaged, while all the moulds have been destroyed! This being a costly work and a matter of more or less national concern, the Author will not refuse subscriptions towards it if any who are interested in the preservation of the Manks Crosses be inclined to share in the expense.

Ramsey, Isle of Man,
March, 1892.

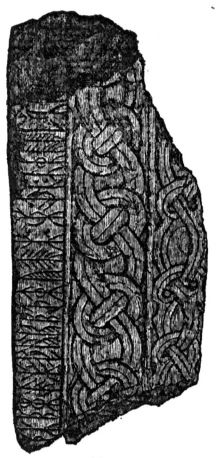

Fig. 1.

BIND RUNE CROSS, ANDREAS (4).

INTRODUCTION.

THE ISLE OF MAN is peculiarly rich in monumental remains of about the 12th century, erected for the most part by the Scandinavians who then occupied the land. It is difficult to assign a precise date, but probably those which bear the names of Norse sculptors such as Gaut, Thorbjörn, and Thurith, may be subsequent to the visit of Magnus Barefoot, King of Norway, who in 1098 arrived to find the Island well-nigh depopulated by internecine strife, and who, as we learn from the Chronicon Manniæ and other sources, encouraged new colonists to come over from Norway, and formed large settlements in Man and the Isles. But the custom of erecting crosses as memorials to their dead had prevailed among the Celtic inhabitants before their pagan invaders first arrived, and the art of decorating them with elaborate geometric designs had doubtless made considerable progress before the Norsemen, who had now adopted the religion of the earlier inhabitants, adopted also their custom of raising these sepulchral monuments. Some very primitive looking ancient slabs are still to be met with in out of the way places, and many no doubt are lost or destroyed; there are also a few of later date and a different character, but, the greater number appear to belong to the early part of the 12th century.

In the following Catalogue these have been arranged according to the parishes in which they have been respectively discovered, and to which let us hope those which have been removed may yet be returned, the parishes being arranged in alphabetical order. The most simple in design and ornamentation, which in many instances are no doubt also the earliest, are placed first in each parish, followed in order by others as they grow more complex or conventional.

References are made to the illustrations in Cumming's "Runic Remains," which unfortunately, however, are often inaccurate; very few others have been published, and they are not generally accessible. The descriptions are pretty full—the Author trusts also clear—his object being not only to allow the crosses to be identified, but to help the reader to classify them by the ornamentation, and to enable those who have not seen the Crosses to form some idea of their beauty, character, and general appearance.

The slabs, except Nos. 24 and 25 in the Catalogue, are all of the local rock, clay-slate, in some cases tough and blue, in others running into trap and harder than granite; generally it is evident that the stone has been procured in the immediate neighbourhood. The designs are for the most part sculptured in low relief. When *incised* the fact is expressly mentioned in the Catalogue. In all instances the Inscriptions are incised, and, being generally on the edge, are much injured and rendered difficult to decipher owing to the cracks and seams in the stone caused by exposure to the weather, which makes it sometimes impossible to distinguish more than the line of the stem of a Rune; it is evident, however, that had they been carved on the face, the same amount of weathering would have completely obliterated them, as in too many cases it has the pattern. The terms "Runic" and "Rune" are frequently mis-applied. The Runes are simply the characters in which these inscriptions are carved, and have nothing to do with the language, which, in the Manks inscriptions is Scandinavian of the 12th century. To speak of a stone which bears an inscription in runes as a *Runic Stone* is as though we should call a modern tombstone a *Roman Stone* because the inscription is carved in Roman capitals. As to the origin and development of Runes the reader should consult Canon Isaac Taylor's admirable little book "Greeks and Goths," where their origin is clearly traced to a Greek source, namely the Thracian or Second Ionian Alphabet, which through the intercourse of the Greek colonists at the mouth of the Danube with the Goths south of the Baltic, was introduced in a modified form into Northern Europe, and, had become established as a Runic Futhork certainly as early as the Christian era. The main stages of development are classified by Canon Taylor as the Gothic, the Anglian, and the Scandinavian. The Manks runes clearly belong to the latter, but, as might be expected from the isolated position of Man, show some slight diversities, both of form and value, of which the following are the most characteristic: the form for E is with us a stung-rune, i.e., an I with a central dot; the form for S is a half stem ending in a dot; that for B is the Scandinavian O, with the twigs on the left side only of the stem; and O has the twigs on the right side of the stem and falling from left to right. It has always been held that H—hagal, is absent, but Canon Taylor in the *Academy* [March 12th, 1887, No. 775] takes an N-form in one of the inscriptions to stand for H, the twig on the left side broken off. The writer would suggest that the same form as used for E served also for H. Professor Stephens, to whom he would here record his grateful acknowledgments for kind and valuable assistance in deciphering many of the inscriptions, informs him that all forms from the stung-rune to the fully developed hagal may be met with in various inscriptions; and in this way can be explained the spelling of EIN, or, as here given, HIN—*THE*, and the like. The runes in all the inscriptions are of the same form, allowing for difference of workmanship, of material, and of space; but there is one exception. On a slab at Michael, 62 in the Catalogue, are two legends, both of which have the following four runes differently formed:—S, which is the usual Scandinavian S turned backwards, and N, A, T, which have their respective twigs on both sides of the stem instead of one only, and, with regard to N and A, finished by dots deeply punctured. There is, however, one other important exception, namely, the Andreas slab, 4 in the Catalogue, which is the only instance yet met with in Man of the Bind-runes, i.e., three or four runes having one stem in common, and forming, in fact, a monogram. But the Ornamentation of the Manks Crosses is as interesting as the Inscriptions. A regular development may be observed from the most simple Plait and Twist to the most complex and beautiful geometric designs, and from the geometric to the zoomorphic. A striking feature is the realistic and admirably drawn forms of birds and beasts of the chase and of men, though the latter are not generally a success, occasionally the human form with heads of birds, or wings. Of course this is not the place to give a detailed account of the patterns, but the author cannot help drawing attention to the very beautiful developments of the Twist pattern in especial, culminating in the lovely Loop-form on one face of 4, and in what he has ventured to call the Tendril-pattern as seen in 4, 9, 20, 61, and others, these forms being moreover peculiar to the Isle of Man. Besides the purely decorative work, we are fortunate in having on three of our Cross slabs illustrations from the old Norse Sagas, namely the story of Fafni's Bane, which is represented on stones at Andreas, Jurby, and Malew—Nos. 5, 39, and 47, in the Catalogue. At Andreas, Sigurd is shown roasting the heart of the Dragon Fafni, which he holds on a spit over the fire with one hand, his other being raised to his mouth; behind him are figured his horse Grana and one of the Talking Birds. Below is another figure of Sigurd in the act of stabbing the Dragon. On the Jurby Cross the Dragon is the main feature, Sigurd crouched under him, running his sword through his body. Below is another figure of Sigurd with his thumb in his mouth. At Malew, Sigurd again appears roasting the heart over the fire. Scriptural subjects are almost absent, but on a large Cross at Braddan, 14, is a representation of Daniel in the Lion's Den, and at Bride, on a slab which appears, however, not to have been part of a Cross, 25, is a mediæval carving of the Fall of Adam, a peculiarity of which is the absence of the Serpent.

The slabs themselves are in general rectangular, sometimes having the upper corners rounded off, and sometimes the whole head in what has been called a Wheel-cross. Occasionally the spaces between the limbs and the surrounding circle are pierced, and, in a few instances, the slab is itself cruciform. Usually both faces are sculptured, and in all cases the cross is the chief, if not the only feature. This is of the type known as " Celtic," *i.e.*, a modified Maltese cross within a circle, but having the shaft prolonged and the other limbs generally projecting slightly beyond the circle. The great number and variety of modified forms of this type are a study in themselves.

The writer hopes before long to be able to publish a work now for some time in preparation, giving a full description and account of all these beautiful Crosses, with a large-sized Plate of each face and edge of every one of them, from photographs taken by Mr Patterson, of Ramsey. There are, however, known to be some still built into

Churches and walls, and he is anxious to include figures of them, as well as of any others which may be brought to light. Meanwhile this little Catalogue may be of use and interest both to residents and to students and antiquaries, who may not have such opportunities of seeing the actual Crosses. If it serve to arouse an additional interest in them, and promote ever so little the movement for their protection from weather and from accidents, he will be well repaid the trouble of preparing it—a trouble which is a great deal more than the size or appearance of the work might lead a stranger to suppose, but, at the same time, is with him a labour of love.

Of all the antiquities in which our Island is so rich, our ancient Crosses appeal most strongly to our feelings for protection with a loving care. Their original purpose and venerable age, their historical associations, and their artistic merits, demand at our hands a better treatment than they have met with; and though we cannot now restore or improve them, we can prevent their further injury and decay, and can at least hand down to those who come after us the fragments that are left us.

"And those quaint old fragments that are left us,
  Have their power in this,—the carver brought
Earnest care, and reverent patience, only
  Worthily to clothe some noble thought."

Fig. 2.

FAFNI'S BANE, ANDREAS, 5.

CATALOGUE OF MANKS CROSSES.

ANDREAS.

WITHIN THE SOUTH PORCH OF THE CHURCH.

(1) I. (CUMMING, Fig. 10.) Formerly on the Green in front of the Church, a rectangular slab measuring 8ft 1½in. by 17in. to 18in. wide and 5in. thick. Each face with shafted cross and circle. *Ornament*, the shaft on either face with Plait of five cords, the spaces right and left of the shaft having on one face Twist and a loop-form of the Tendril pattern, and on the other face, Twist-and-ring, and the Key-pattern. *Inscription* up one edge.

(2) II. A fragment, 24in. by 9in. and 4½in thick. On each face the foot of a shafted cross. *Ornament*, on one face the Vertebral and Key-patterns, on the other Twist and Interlacing.

(3) III. A fragment, formerly in the Rectory yard, 17in. by 24in. and 2½in. thick. One face chipped away, the other with remains of Interlacing, apparently on a portion of the shaft of a cross.

(4) IV. A fragment, 22¼in. by 10½in. and 2⅜in. thick. *Ornament*, one face, on the shaft the Tendril pattern, space to the right Key pattern; the other face Twist-and-ring on the shaft, a loop form of Tendril pattern to the right, and, running up space to the left, *Inscription* in Bind-Runes. [See Fig. 1.]

(5) V. A fragment, 2ft. 3in. by 1ft. 4in. and 3in. thick. Each face with portion of shaft of cross and part of circle surrounding its head. *Ornament*, Interlacing merging into Zoomorphic. On one face, shaft with dragon interlacement; space to the left, representation of Sigurd roasting the heart of the dragon Fafni; above, his horse Grana

B

and one of the talking birds; below, another dragon with interlacing and Sigurd with a sword stabbing it. [See Fig. 2.] The other face, on the shaft, a robed figure, probably Loki, manacled, attacked by a serpent. A strange mixture of Christian symbolism and illustrations of the Sagas and ancient Northern Mythology. [See Fig. 3.]

(6) VI. (CUMMING, Fig. 9.) A rectangular slab 6ft. 3½ by 15in. and 4½ to 5½in. thick. Each face with cross but no surrounding circle. *Ornament*, one face has on the shaft a Plait of four cords bordered by Key and Step-patterns, and, on either side, figures of birds and beasts; the other has the Vertebral pattern on the shaft, birds, beasts, and serpents at either side, with peculiar square knotwork; below the cross, a robed figure seated side-ways on horseback, in front of which is a band with Tendril-pattern. Beneath this the figure of a hound *incised*. *Inscription* up one edge.

(7) VII. A fragment, 14in. by 7½in. and 2¼in. thick. Each face shows a limb, and portions of the shaft of a cross without surrounding circle. *Ornament*, on shaft, both faces, Vertebral pattern, and, at the side which remains, square knotwork, human figures, beasts, birds, and serpents. *Inscription* running *down* one edge. [See Figs. 4, 5, 6.]

(8) VIII. A fragment, 2ft. 10in. by 7in. and 3in. thick. One face chipped away. The other with traces of the head and shaft of a cross as in 6 and 7. *Ornament*, shaft with Vertebral pattern, space to right with Plait. *Inscription* up one edge.

In the Churchyard is a slab showing, on one face, the *drawing* of a Cross never carved. The other face has been utilized as a modern tombstone.

BALLAUGH.

(9) I. (CUMMING, Fig. 2.) Within the Old Church, a slab with rounded head and expanding base measuring 4ft. 6in. by 20in. across the head, 14in. across fust, and 18in. across the base; and 3in. thick. Each face with shafted cross surrounded in one case by the usual circle. *Ornament*, on one face, no surrounding circle; above the arms two lozenges interlaced, joined over the head, and finished by elaborate flourishes; the head with pelleted

ribbons interlacing round a central boss and breaking into the Tendril pattern on the shaft, the space to the left is occupied by the Key pattern, and that to the right by the Vertebral pattern terminated by a small cross. The other face has a plait of pelleted ribbons round a central boss, breaking on the shaft, into a very elaborate loop-form of Tendril pattern with pelleted rings round the loop and interlaced with it. The space to the right with plait of four cords, that to the left being occupied by the *Inscription*, which terminates in the cavity between the arms and the surrounding circle.

BRADDAN.

(10) I. Set up on a mound about 8 yards south of the Church, a broken slab about 35½in. by 5½in to 6½in., and 6in. thick. One face with remains of shafted cross and circle in relief, plain and very rudely carved. The cross has the angles at the junction of the limbs without the usual cup-like hollows, but the limbs expand.

(11) II. (CUMMING, Fig. 38.) In the Churchyard, set up near the stile at the north-west corner, a slab 29in. above the surface of the ground by 19in. wide and 2½in. thick; one face a cross pateé, plain, the lower limb extending beyond the raised circle which encloses the other limbs. In the centre an *incised* circle.

(12) III. In Churchyard on mound with 10, a rectangular slab 3ft. 10in. above the ground by 17in. and 2in. to 4in. thick. Each face with shafted cross and circle. One is almost entirely worn away, but shows by way of *Ornament* on one side of the shaft traces of the Key-pattern; the other face has on the shaft the Vertebral pattern, and to the left of it a plait of four cords, the space to the right being occupied by the *Inscription*. The head is unfortunately broken off just above the centre. It seems to have borne a novel and beautiful design of four bands at right angles to four other bands, interplaited in the centre, and looped heart-shaped rings at the extremities.

(13) IV. (CUMMING, Fig. 12.) Now in Mr Wallace's Museum, Distington, a fragment 15½in. by 9in. by 3½in. Each face with remains of head of cross without surrounding circle. *Ornament*, interlaced lozenges slightly foliated. *Inscription* running up the shaft of the cross and space to the left of the head.

(14) V. (CUMMING, Fig. 21.) Set against south wall of Church, round-headed slab, the head 38in. diameter. The fust, which is 7in. out of the ground, is 23in. across. *Ornament*, continuous interlacing on the cross excepting the upper limb, which bears two animals supporting a mask between them. Between the limbs, each segment has, betwixt raised borders ornamented with a plait of four cords, the figure of some beast.

(15) VI. (CUMMING, Fig. 16.) In Churchyard, set up beside 11, a slab with rounded head but limbs slightly projecting, 5ft. 6in. above the ground (4in. below) by 13in. across the neck, and 17in. across the widest part, and 3 to 3½in. thick. *Ornament*, one face, shaft with looped plait — not elsewhere found on the Manks Crosses. Head with knotwork within a circle of Twist-and-ring pattern—the spaces between the limbs pierced. The reversed face shows an *incised* cross and remains of circle.

(16) VII. (CUMMING, Fig. 23.) On mound with 10, the broken shaft of a pillar cross 3ft. 8in. above the surface, 7½in. wide where broken off, increasing to 12in. at the surface of the ground, and 3 to 3½in. thick. *Ornament*, one face, two pelleted dragons with knotwork more foliated than on the next, a border with step-pattern below and a flat *bordered* rope-pattern on either side; the other face a plait of six cords in a panel, below, a panel of elaborate knotwork, the panels divided by bands having the step-pattern, a smooth raised border at either side. One edge is occupied by the step-pattern, the other by the *Inscription*, both having raised borders.

(17) VIII. (CUMMING, Fig. 22.) In Churchyard, set up on mound with the last, a monolith rectangular pillar cross, 4ft. 8in. above the surface (4 to 6in. below); 9½in. across the head (the total width of which when perfect was about 12in.)—5¾in. across the neck, increasing to 9in. at the surface of the ground; thickness 3⅓in at the neck, increasing to 5¾in. at the surface. *Ornament*, one face—the head bears an equal-limbed cross with four bands plaited across its centre, surrounded by circle ornamented by the Twist pattern—the spaces between the limbs pierced; on the fust are four pelleted dragons, interlaced with intricate knotwork. The other face is very similar. One edge has

a single dragon from top to bottom with similar interlacing. The *Inscription* runs up the other edge. Each face is bordered by ropework moulding.

(18) IX. In Government Office; a fragment from Baldwin, 21in. by 10in. by 3in. Plain, except that it bears remains of *Inscription* running up the middle of one face.

(19) X. In Mr Wallace's museum, Distington, a fragment dug up by Lieut. Charlton in his garden adjoining the Churchyard. It measures 6½in. by 1¾in. by ¼in., and appears to have been flaked off the face (about the centre) of a Cross similar to, if not identical with 13. It shows by way of *Ornament* the remains of two crossed bands pelleted.

(20) XI. (CUMMING, Fig. 39.) Now lost. Appears to have been perfect when seen by Kinnebrook, who figures it, but does not mention it in his descriptive letter-press. To judge from his Figure (21) the total length of the stone (by comparison with one alongside which it stands) might be about two feet; diameter of circle about 12 in. It bore simply a linear Cross within a circle, with a small circle between each limb, all *incised*.

On the west gable of the Church is a small cross, having on the east-face a crucifix.

BRIDE.

IN THE CHURCH PORCH.

(21) I. A slab, 3ft. 8in. by 1ft. 2in. and 2in. thick. Both faces show lower portion of shaft of cross. *Ornament*, shaft with plait of five cords, the space to the left having four ribbons interplaited with diamond-shaped rings, breaking into the Key-pattern on the portion now lost; that to the right a beautiful development of the Loop or Tendril-pattern, and the figure of an animal; the other face has on the shaft the Vertebral pattern, to the right of it the Tendril and to the left a repetition of the Loop-pattern. *Inscription* running up one edge.

(22) II. A fine slab rounded at the top, 5ft. 6in. by 1ft. 9in. and 3in. thick. Each face with equal-limbed cross within circle, the spaces between the limbs pierced. *Ornament*, one face Twist-and-ring, Key-pattern, and Plait-of-four running one into the other round the circle; the limbs with an irregular Key-pattern, the lower one

with a Plait-of-four; above the circle, a panel with
diagonal Key-pattern (with Step-pattern border), at either
side of which incised figure of a man and a triangle; below the circle, a panel with similar Key-pattern with a
rope-border, from the panel to the bottom a band down
the middle with Step-pattern; to the right of this the
figure of a man, with a spiral device above his shoulder;
below, a plait-of-nine, below a horse or stag (the back
broken off) with figures of men, two seated and one
prostrate under him; to the left of the band, the figure of
a bird, below, a man by the side of which a coiled ropework serpent; below, a small figure of a man; below,
a man with arms a-kimbo and legs outspread, the spaces
between his limbs being filled with knotwork; below a
Step-pattern border and square of diagonal Key-pattern;
below, a double volute from right to left.   There are three
small Triquetras in the patterns; both sides of this face are
bordered by a parallel rope and a step-pattern.   The other
face has, round the circle Twist-and Ring pattern, and, on
the limbs of the Cross knot-work and compressed diagonal
Key-pattern; above the circle a panel with diagonal Key-
pattern, at either side a cock, and a Triquetra (that to
the left broken off), below the circle a panel with double
spirals from which a narrow band runs down the middle,
having the Vertebral pattern; to the right of this band
the figure of a Man with a Net, over his left shoulder an
∽-shaped device; below a bird and a stag, ornamented
with interlaced work, and having a knot between its
limbs,—at back and front of which is a hound; below,
a square of diagonal Key-pattern; below, two hounds
with collars—the rest is broken off.   To the left of the
band the figure of a Bird, a Man with a spear, and a Stag;
under the Stag a Man with a knife, at its back a hound,
below another hound and Key-pattern, the whole has a
border of Step-pattern, outside of which is a rope-border,
terminating at the right in a Serpent's head.

(23) III. (CUMMING, FIG. 6.) In Mr Wallace's museum,
Distington, a fragment, 1ft. 3½in. by 9in., showing dragon-
head and interlaced work.   Removed from the Churchyard about 1840.

(24) IV. (CUMMING, Fig. 41.) In the Porch. The
broken shaft of a small pillar-cross of new red sandstone,
23in. above the ground (original length about 4ft.), 15in

wide at the base and 10in. above; 7in. thick. Unfortunately the head is now broken off and lost; it appears as etched by Kinnebrook in 1841, to have been cruciform in shape and ornamented merely by *incised* circles in each limb, connected one with the other by straight lines; a line also joins the upper and lower circles, the latter being further connected by lines running to the angles below each arm of the cross. A careful examination convinces me that it has been ornamented with a plait on the same face.

(25) V. In the Porch. A square slab of sandstone measuring 12in. high by 14in. wide, with a representation of the Temptation. Adam to the right and Eve to the left, in profile, the Tree without overhanging branches, and no Serpent.

Many pieces of "picture stones" I am informed by one of the masons concerned, were broken deliberately and built into the present Church.

CONCHAN.

(26) I. (CUMMING, Fig. 26). In S. Catherine's garden, a loose slab shaped not unlike the lid of a coffin, 3ft. 9in. by 1ft. 7in. and 2in. thick. Each face with a plain *incised* cross and circle,—an equal-limbed within a shafted cross. *Inscription* irregularly over the surface of both faces.

(27) II. (CUMMING, Fig. 25.) In Churchyard north side of tower, a rectangular slab 4ft. 7in. above the ground, by 2ft. 3in. and 6 to 6½in. thick. Each face with *incised* shafted cross and circle. *Ornament*, one face, a plain circle on head of cross, with limbs expanding, and having a plain border; a fillet forming a square by passing over the face of the cross and under and over the circle in heart-shaped loops between the limbs; the shaft has a design of four bands interplaited with diamond-shaped rings, the other face with five bosses, one in the centre and four between the limbs of the cross outside the circle. The shaft with interlaced design.

(28) III. (CUMMING, Fig. 17.) In Churchyard, a slab with rounded top 4ft. 6in. above the ground, by 1ft. 7in. wide and 3½in. thick. One face with shafted cross and circle. *Ornament*, on cross and circle a continuous plait of

10 cords,—at either side of shaft a grotesque animal with
volutes and scrolls, a band of scroll-ornament below the
shaft.   Below, a Fylfot with spiral termination.

(29) IV.   (CUMMING, Fig. 18.)   In S. Catherine's
garden, a loose fragment 4ft. 11in. by 18in. and 1½in. thick.
Ornament, a sort of looped Figure-of-eight and other plaits
on the cross and circle, dog-headed figure, and spirals.

(30) V.   By the side of 25, a broken slab 2ft. 6in.
above the ground by 14in. and 1½in.   One face with
equal-limbed cross on circle.   *Ornament*, continuous, but
irregular plait on cross, and plait-of-four on circles; below, in sunk panel, figures of beasts, a geometrical device
and one of three pellets in a triangle.

Train makes mention of another stone as being
"at the entrance to the Church," having a "Danish
warrior in complete armour" carved upon it.

In S. Catherine's Garden there is a Gable Cross
on the gable of the old Church which is there set up.

GERMAN.

(31) I.   In the Cathedral, Peel, are some slabs with
incised linear crosses on their faces, otherwise quite plain,
namely in the west wall of the north transept one
measuring 3ft. 9in. by 20in., with a Latin cross, the head
terminated by two small circles, and four circles between
the limbs.

(32) II.   In the same wall, a slab 15in. by 12in., with
cross pateé, the upper and lower limbs about twice the
thickness of the other two.

(33) III.   In the east wall of the same transept, a slab
9in by 18in., having a somewhat similar cross to the
last, but the shaft more prolonged.

(34) IV.   (CUMMING, Fig. 5.)   In porch of S. John's
Church, a fragment 3ft. 9in. by 15in., and 4 to 4½in. thick.
One face sculptured showing lower portion of shaft of
cross.   *Ornament*, Vertebral pattern on the shaft. one edge
shows traces of Twist or Twist-and-ring pattern.   *Inscription* up the other edge.

(35) V.   In the Guard-house, Peel Castle, a fragment,
18in. by 4 to 7½in. and 1¼in. thick, showing on one face
the remains of a shafted cross and circle with interlaced
design.   The other face chipped off.

(36) VI. (Cumming, Fig. 27.) Fragment built into wall of the Cathedral, 2ft. 3in. long and 2in. thick. The remains of the *Inscription* on one edge is all that is visible.

Near Cronk-ny-Keeillane was a cross which many years ago was buried, as it was supposed to have caused a murrain among the cattle. It is to this Mr Kneale refers when he says in his Guide (p. 124): "Some years ago a slab engraven with characters which no one can decipher was dug up in this parish."

JURBY.

(37) I. In the Treen Chapel, West Nappin, a slab measuring 17in. by 12in., by 1½ to 1¾in thick. *Incised* upon one face, an equal-limbed cross formed by two lines at right angles, having diagonal lines to mark the expansion at the extremities of the limbs.

(38) II. At the West Nappin Chapel, a broken slab of which two portions have been recovered from the gable wall into which they were formerly built; one measures 6ft. 3in. by 11in. to 9in. wide at a distance of two feet from the top from which it tapers to a point, and 3½ to 5in. thick; the other 4ft. 1in. by 8in. by 4in. On each face has been a shafted cross with circle. The larger piece shows on one face the remains of the shaft with a Plait-of-five, to the left elaborate interlacing, the circle is plain with moulded borders; on the other face the shaft is flaked off except a few inches at the bottom, the space to the right has the Tendril-pattern. The end of the right limb remains, showing a device similar to that of 39, with the diamond-shaped ring pelleted; the portion of the circle between this limb and the shaft bears a Plait-of-four between plain moulded borders. The smaller piece bears on one face the remains of the shaft with Plait-of-five, and on the space to the right the Vertebral-pattern; the other face is entirely flaked away. One edge (Cumming, Fig. 31), formerly exposed inside the ruined gable, bears the Key-pattern.

(39) III. Set up as a Gate-post to a field at the entrance to the Church-yard; a slab 7ft. by 1 -20in. wide and 6½in thick. Each face with remains of shafted cross

and circle. *Ornament*, circle plain with raised borders. To the right a dragon scored, and man piercing him with a sword—another illustration of Fafni's Bane. Below, Sigurd sucking his thumb; below, a horse. The other face is almost worn off but shows left arm of cross, and, near the bottom, remains of the Tendril-pattern.

(40) IV. (Cumming, Fig. 11.) In porch of Church, a fragment 30in. by 16in. and 2in. thick. Each face with head of shafted cross, but no surrounding circle. *Ornament*, one face, plait breaking into a loop-form of Tendril-pattern on the shaft; on space at left side Key-pattern, and on the other side an elaborate loop-form knot; above the left arm of the cross a robed figure, another over the other arm is now broken off. The other face has a Twist of four cords on the shaft, above the arms figures of men (one with a long horn or trumpet issuing from his mouth), the space right of the shaft a curious knot, that to the left with *Inscription* running up and then down.

(41) V. (Cumming, Fig. 7.) In the Church a loose fragment, 31in. by 20in. and 3in. thick. Each face shows the lower portion of shaft of a cross. *Ornament*, shaft with Plait-and-ring, pelleted, as in 33, on the right a Boar, below, a Stag; on the left a robed figure with Trident, below, figure with pole over his shoulder and a man hanging by a rope at the end of it. The other face has on the shaft the Vertebral pattern, to the right a device of pellets surrounded by Step-pattern border, to the left Tendril-pattern.

LEZAYRE.

(42) I. In the Masonic Rooms, Ramsey, a loose fragment 20in. by 14in. and 4in. thick, sculptured on each face with cross and circle in high relief; with bosses in sockets at the junction of the limbs. *Ornament*, one face has a large flat boss in the centre with a beautiful design consisting of a band so turned upon itself as to form a cross surrounded by a double circle; each limb has borne a design but the stone is too broken to make them out. The other face bears in the centre a device of four Triquetras formed by an endless band, and divided by a deeply incised linear cross. One limb has borne a design of two Triquetras round a linear cross; another a circle with an endless band looped round it four times,

LONAN.

(43) I. (CUMMING, Fig. 34.) In Government Office, a round-headed slab broken across the middle: about 5ft. long by 22in. across the head, and 14in. tapering to 12in. across the fust, and 3in. thick. One face with plain shafted cross (with pedestal) and circles.

(44) II. (CUMMING, Fig. 40.) At Glionroy farm-house, a loose fragment 1ft. 3in. by 10in. wide and 4in. thick. In an adjoining farm the rest of the cross is at present built as a lintel over the stable door. It was correctly figured by Kinnebrook (14), but very badly by Cumming. The former gives the dimensions as 3ft. 2½in. (this would be as it stood with the head broken off), by 20in. wide. One face had shafted cross and circles, the shaft terminating in two volutes between which two triangles of three pellets each.

(45) III. In old Parish Church, a loose fragment of Silurian grit 18in. by 18in. and 5in. thick at the top. One face with portion of head of cross upon circle. In the centre a small boss in a socket.

(46) IV. (CUMMING, Fig. 20.) In old Churchyard, a round-headed slab 5ft. 5in. above the ground, by 3ft. 2in. wide; one face with equal-limbed cross upon two circles in relief. *Ornament*, continuous plait on the cross and plaits of four and three on the segments of the circles, the spaces between the circles have designs of lozenges interlaced. Below, four bands across the fust, with plaits alternately of four and three.

MALEW.

(47) I. (CUMMING, Fig. 15.) In Churchyard, near the entrance, a broken slab 5ft. by 1ft. 6in. and 2in. to 3in. thick. Each face with shaft of cross. *Ornament*, one face—shaft with dragon-headed knotwork and, at either side interlacing; the other shaft with Twist-and-ring breaking into a plait; at the right side, figure of Sigurd (as pointed out by Prof. G. F. Browne) armed with a sword, and holding on a spit the heart of the dragon Fafni; below, separated by a broad band, an elaborate knot; at the left, figure of a horse broken off at the neck; below, separated by a band, some device now broken off.

MAROWN.

(48) I. (CUMMING, Fig. 45. Bad and misleading figure.)
" S. Patrick's Chair." At Margher-y-Chiarn, the Garth,
two stones set on a mound which measures 7ft. long by
4ft. deep, and 18in. high. One of them, 3ft. 6in. above
the surface, by 16 to 22in. wide, bears, on one face, a plain,
incised, equal-limbed Cross. The other, 2ft. 11in, by about
12 to 10in. wide, has a similar Cross. Another long stone
lies against one end of the mound, but appears to have no
carving on it.

MAUGHOLD.

(49.) I. On the wall of Cabbal Keeil Woirrey, Corna,
a slab 3ft. 6in. by 1ft. 6in., tapering to a point. On one
face an incised linear Latin cross measuring 12in. by 10in.
There is a faint appearance as of circles between the
limbs, as on that at Peel, and at Braddan.

(50) II. In Churchyard, against the wall at the north
door, a cruciform slab 4ft. 9in. by 12in. and 3in. thick.
One face carved, having a boss in the centre ; down the
middle of the shaft, between a band (waved at the top
in five curves) in relief, and another 12 in. lower down,
formed by two incised lines, are five small circular holes
two inches apart. The right arm is broken.

(51) III. In Churchyard, with the last, a fragment
19in. by 14in and 2½in. thick, having on one face remains
of a cross *incised*, the limbs joined by a narrow band
giving the appearance of bosses at their junction, apparently no ornamentation.

(52) IV. With the last, a slab about 3ft. 2in. by 1ft.
7in. and 4in. thick. On one face a cross pateé within a
circle, no ornament but a narrow border.

(53) V. (CUMMING, Fig. 36.) In Churchyard about 20
yards south of porch, a plain round-headed slab, 4ft. above
the ground, the diameter of circle 2ft. 6in., width of fust
16 to 8in, thickness 4in. tapering to 3in. On one face a
cross pateé on a broad flat circle, surmounted by a moulded
border; below, a panel formed by incised lines. The other
face has the outer moulding or rim of circle and panel
below, but no cross.

(54) VI. (CUMMING, Fig. 37.) Set up on the hedge by
the side of the high-road at Port-y-Vullin, a rectangular
slab, but top corners rounded off, 6ft. above the surface

by 3ft. wide at the top, tapering to 2ft. 3in. and 5in. thick. One face sculptured, having shafted cross—with pedestal—and circle, deeply *incised;* the centre occupied by raised boss, and within the circle, at the points where it is over-lapped by the limbs, are four smaller bosses, the space between them and the centre being quite plain, so that in fact the actual cross is merely *suggested.*

(55) VII. In Churchyard, against wall at north door a slab 4ft. 9in. long by 10-11in. and 3-3½in. thick, broken but showing a rounded head ornamented by a beautiful hexagonal device *incised,* and below this a cross deeply *incised.*

(56) VIII. At Ballaglass a slab 2ft. 6in. by 13½in. by 4in., having on one face a cross pateé and circle, plain, the upper limb extended above the circle and the shaft below. The cross is bordered by an incised line which terminates in a dot at either side of the shaft a few inches from the end.

(57) IX. On the Ard Cooillean, near the Rhennee, Dhoon, a rectangular slab, broken across, measuring 2ft. 10in. by 1ft. 10in. by about 2in. On one face are the faint remains of a Celtic cross and circle, plain.

(58) X. In the Masonic Rooms, Ramsey, a slab from Cabbal Keeil Woirey, Corna, 2ft. 4in. by 1ft. by 2in., rough and broken. One face bears an *Inscription,* in two lines, very rudely cut.

(59) XI. (CUMMING, Fig. 33.) Now in Malew Church-yard (having been removed by Mr Cumming to King William's College, and thence recently to Malew), a loose fragment 4ft. 4in. by 1ft. 4in.; one face carved showing portion of the shaft and one arm of cross upon circle. *Ornament* on shaft, Plait-and-ring.

(60) XII. Set up against west gable of Church, a rectangular slab 4ft. 4in. by 12in. and 4in. thick. Each face with shafted cross and circle, once covered by a con-tinuous plait of which but the faintest traces now remain.

(61) XIII. Set up against south pillar of Church gates, a rectangular slab 4ft. 5in. above the ground by 1ft. 9½in., reduced at the surface to 1ft. 8in., and 4in. thick. One face with shafted cross—square-centred, with pedestal—and circle. *Ornament,* interlaced pattern on cross and circle now all but completely worn away.

(62) XIV. Set up against north pillar, a slab about 7ft. 6in. by 2ft. 5in., tapering to 12in , and 3 to 4in. thick. One face with a large shafted cross upon circle, the shaft attached at the other end to a smaller circle containing an equal-limbed cross. *Ornament*, continuous plaits on cross and circles, now almost worn away.

(63) XV. In the Church, a round-headed slab 1ft. 9in. by 9in. and 3in. thick. The edges of one face bevelled. Each face with equal-limbed cross on a circle ; below, a wider shaft. *Ornament*, one face, plait-of-eight on shaft which is in relief and edged with a cable moulding, and plaits in the square ends of the limbs, the circle with step-pattern ; the other, Vertebral pattern on the shaft and irregular plaits in the square ends of limbs, between which the circle shows Plaits-of-four, two ending in the head of a serpent.

(64) XVI. A loose fragment at the steps to the north entrance, 2ft. by 1ft. 5in. and 3½in. One face with cross and circle, the angles at the arms without the hollow cup-like depressions ; the centre chiselled out in form of a minor cross. which may have had a crucifix or figure of the Virgin and Child. *Ornament*, knotwork and plait. A portion of the border remains to show that the whole was included in a panel.

(65) XVII. Against the west gable of the Church, a round-headed slab broken off at 2ft. 10in.; 18in. wide, (12in. across the top of the fust) and 4in. thick. The upper part with cross pateé surrounded by a plain moulding. In the centre two circles with plaits of three cords, each of the limbs with separate knotwork device. Below the circle, figure of a man, nude or in tight fitting garments, with the limbs spread out.

(66) XVIII. Against the west gable of the Church, a rectangular slab 4ft. 6in. by 20in. and 2in. thick. One face with shafted cross and circle. *Ornament*, plait formerly covering cross and circle now entirely worn away. Below the circle, at either side of the shaft the figure of a monk seated on a stool, below, man on horseback, below, a boar and other animal.

(67) XIX. Lintel over the west entrance to the Church, 5ft. by 9-10in. and 5in. thick, broken along the entire length. One face alone visible. Half its length occupied by shaft of cross terminated by volutes and having plait of

four cords; the space left of shaft with robed figure having peaked beard facing shaft. The lower half with figures of stags and hounds.

(68) XX. In the middle of the Green before the Church-gates, a rectangular slab 6ft. 9in. above the surface, by 1ft. 9in. wide and 7in. thick. One face occupied by cross with square base, the head being almost as long as the shaft, and circle; on the head of the cross the figure of a man, at his right side a Pastoral staff, above which a scroll device (?), and above, a rope border or some such device; on the shaft the figure of Virgin with nimbus and Child; in the centre a circle formed by the Step-pattern, on either side of which a cock. The space either side of the head occupied by irregular Key-pattern; below are irregular square designs, on the right, almost worn away. The spaces between the limbs are filled in with spirals. The other face bears a cross of somewhat similar form, with a circle, in a panel occupying half its length and bordered by Rope-pattern. Above the circle on the right, Step-pattern and Twist; on the left some incised pattern now worn off; below the circle a plait on the left and irregular angular interlacing on the right. The lower panel is divided by a central line, up the left side of which a procession of four animals, perhaps Deer, followed by Dogs, and irregular scroll-work; at the right is a man on horseback—resting his enormous head on the horse's neck, twist and angular work. One edge has an *incised* pattern consisting of disconnected curves having the appearance of a Twist, below which are two anchor-like figures and some cross lines like a rudimentary plait. The other edge has at the top an *incised* diagonal Key pattern, below. two lozenges interlaced, incised scroll-like figures, a peculiar knot and loop, and a plait of three double cords with pellets at the sides.

(69) XXI. Built as a lintel over East window, a slab about 6ft. long by 13in. wide, with rude figures of man and animals on one face.

(70) XXII. In Government Office, a loose fragment, from Ballagilley, measuring 8in. by 7in. and 1in thick; one face chipped away, the other showing the forepart of a boar—doubtless one of a number of figures on the space one side of the shaft of a cross. The edge shows remains of four runes, too broken to decipher.

On a large Boulder, near S. Maughold's Well, is a small incised Latin cross.

Two or three other fragments are known to have been built into the walls of the Church.

(Cumming, Fig. 42.) At the entrance to the Church-yard of the Parish Church is a pillar-cross of the 14th century, of old red sandstone. Basement of three steps 9in., 8in., and 14in. high—the upper one 27in. square. Shaft, octagonal, 4ft. 11½in. by 8⅓-9in. Entablature 3ft. high by 14in. square. Above the moulding of the square capital are four shields, bearing, in relief, the first a chalice, the next a circle with a cross above it, enclosing a rosette, the next a square device which Cumming takes for a book, below which is an oak leaf, and the last the Trie Cassyn or Three Legs conjoined—the earliest instance of the use of this device in sculpture in the Island. Above the latter shield is a canopied niche, trefoil, cusped, having a sculptured crucifix; on the opposite side a similar niche, cinquefoil, contains a figure of the Virgin and Child; the canopies of both niches crocketted and finialled; on the other sides are, a kneeling figure, and an oak leaf with rosettes. Above these are two smaller shields, the one with a rosette, the other with three oak leaves and a chief wavy.

I have just seen a Gable Cross of a light yellow sandstone, found in pulling down a wall at the Church gates. It measures 13½in. by 9½in. by 5½in. The head and left arm are broken off, the rest shows remains of a Crucifix much worn.

MICHAEL.

(71) I. (Cumming, Fig. 4.) Within the Church tower, a broken slab 4ft. 3in. by 11½in. and 2½in. thick. Each face with the lower portion of shaft of a cross. *Ornament,* on one face the Vertebral pattern on shaft; to the right a plain twist with pellets between the cords, to the left a form of the Tendril-pattern, with a small angular waved line between the cords. The other face has on the shaft a Twist-with-ring of very broad bands, terminating curiously with scroll-like flourishes, this is almost completely worn away; to the right Key-pattern, at the other side the remains of the *Inscription.*

(72) II. (CUMMING, Fig. 1.) Set in wall south of Church-gates, a rectangular slab 3ft. 8in. above the surface, by 16in. and 3-3½in. thick. Each face with shafted cross and circle. *Ornament*, one face, shaft with Plait of five; to the left, Twist-and-ring, to the right, a loop-form of Tendril-pattern; above the circle at either side two lozenges crossed and interlaced. The other face has on the shaft the Vertebral pattern, the space to the left with a Plait-of-four, that to the right the Tendril-pattern; the *Inscription*, which runs up one edge, terminates above the circle of this face.

(73) III. (CUMMING, Fig. 28.) On wall north of the Church-gates, a rectangular slab 5ft. 9½in. by 17in., tapering to 14in., and 3-4in. thick. One face sculptured, having shafted cross and circle. *Ornament*, interlaced work in panels, the square end of the head and arms having each a design of four Triquetras conjoined. In the centre a disc surrounded by Rope-pattern, outside of which is a beautiful ring of the Vertebral pattern, between which and the Triquetras two lozenges with a square ring. The shaft is occupied by plaits arranged in panels; the cross and circle bordered with the rope-pattern terminating in the head and tail of a serpent. The space to the left of the shaft contains a stag attacked by a hound, below, a robed figure, the left hand raised, the right resting on his sword; that to the right has immediately below the circle an animal like a lamb, below, a harper in tight-fitting garments playing on his harp of four strings; below, a long robed figure standing with left hand extended. There are two *Inscriptions* in runes on the other face, each beginning at the bottom of the slab and running up it. Between these is an Ogham Inscription, and, on the sculptured face an Ogham Alphabet.

(74) IV. (CUMMING, Fig. 3.) Within the tower, two loose fragments, one 25in. by 16in. and 3in. thick, the other 18in. by 14in. and 2½in. thick; the original height of the slab must have been over five feet. Each face bore a shafted cross and circle, a small portion of the latter remaining on the smaller piece. In the way of *Ornament*, one face has on the shaft Plait-and-ring, the ring and the outer band pelleted; left of the shaft Twist-and-ring breaks into a simple plait; on the right we find the Tendril pattern fully developed. The other face has, on the shaft, the Vertebral pattern; to the left, at the top, figure of a man

with nimbus, below this have been three other figures of men—one upside down—with beaks like birds, and below, a boar ; on the other side is a boar followed by a hound, a bird-headed man with bare knees, armed with sword and spear, below, a fish. The *Inscription* runs up one edge.

(75) V. (CUMMING, Fig. 13.) On horse-block in front of Church-gates, a rectangular slab 7ft. 4in. above the surface, by 19-20in. wide and 5-7in. thick. Each face with shafted cross and circle. *Ornament*, the cross (with volutes at the foot and where circle joins the shaft) is ornamented by a continuous plait of 8 cords. Each of the four corners is occupied by a Triquetra ; beneath the Volute on either side a beautiful cross with circle, terminating in Triquetra knots; below, a device of four detached Triquetras forming cross and circle, below, on the left side stags and hounds at their backs, at the right a man on horseback followed by a spare horse. Below the cross are two dragon-like figures, pelleted, interlaced with knotwork. Below, separated by a broad band having the step-pattern, a stag with a hound at its back. The other face has, above the cross, the figure of a stag followed by a hound. On the back of the stag a small bird pursued by a falcon. The cross has on the shaft the Plait-and-ring pattern, ornamented by diagonal lines, terminating in spirals at the foot of the shaft. To the left of shaft a man (bearded) on horseback, below, figures of animals ; on the right are figures of animals. On one edge is a Cock, below, Twist with diamond shaped rings, pelleted. The other edge bears the Inscription, and at the top the figure of a warrior, with round shield and spear.

(76) VI. (CUMMING, Fig. 8.) In Church tower, a loose fragment, 18½in. by 17½in. and 3in. Each face shows upper part of cross and circle. *Ornament*, on head, plait of pelleted ribbons and rings, above, at the left a pelleted dragon with top-knot interlaced, at the right a kilted figure attacked by an eagle. The other face has the plait on the head more foliated, in the centre, a figure with nimbus fringed and bearing three small incised crosses, having the arms outspread as if in the act of blessing, below the feet five large pellets ; above the circle on the left the figure of a cock on a branch showing the loop-pattern of 1 ; to the right a winged figure beneath which is a Triquetra. The last three words of the *Inscription* run up one edge.

(77) VII. (CUMMING, Fig. 17.) In the tower, a round-headed slab 4ft. 6½in. by 22in., tapering to 14½in. at the end of the pattern (about 12½in. from the bottom) below which it is broken, and 2½in. thick. Each face with cross and circle, the spaces between the limbs pierced. *Ornament*, very elaborate and rather conventional interlacing on the cross, plait-of-four on the segments of the circle between the limbs; at either side dragon-headed figures with prolonged top-knots and pointed tails. The other face of similar design and appearance. As in the Lezayre cross (42) the tool marks of a *pointed* instrument are very distinct.

Col. Townley in his Journal [vol. I., p. 173] mentions having "rescued" a cross from some rubbish outside the Churchyard, "displaying the figure of some mighty Danish chief in *complete steel*," which he carried "in triumph to Douglas." It should be possible to trace and recover this cross.

PATRICK.

(78) I. At Ballelby, a few yards from the farm-house, a slab, 4ft. 9in. by 2ft. On one face a cross formed by five linear squares, one in the centre, united.

RUSHEN.

(79) I. At Bradda-mooar, a slab 3ft. 2in. by 1ft. 8in. and 3in. thick. One face with equal-limbed cross formed by four square shallow cup-like excavations, each 3½in. in diameter, and 4½in. apart. Within each arm and above and below the other limbs, are four incised lineal crosses, 2½in. by 2½in.

(80) II. (CUMMING, Fig. 14.) At corner of road from Port Erin to Port St. Mary, a rectangular slab 8ft. by 2ft., with shafted cross and circle on each face. *Ornament*, both faces appear to have had continuous plait on the cross, and perhaps on the spaces at sides, but it is now so worn as to make it almost impossible to decipher. Two of the spaces between the limbs are pierced and this seems rather to be the result of accident than design.

(81) III. (CUMMING, Fig. 30.) In the possession of Mrs Quayle, of Castletown, a fragment from the Calf of Man, 2ft. 2in. by 9½in. and 1½in. thick. On one face portion of a panel containing crucifix, at one side a soldier with spear.

Christ is represented with head erect and eyes open, clothed in the "Tunicata Palmatæ," sleeved and reaching to the feet. The soldier with arms bare.

> (CUMMING, Fig. 43.) At Rushen Abbey, a "Coffin-lid," bearing in relief an elaborate shafted cross with a sword by its side.

SANTON.

(82) I. A slab of about Seventh Century, 3ft. 9in. by 9in. and 4½in. thick, now in Government Office. One face bears a deeply cut *Inscription*, in Roman Capitals.

(83) II. Slab from Ballacorris, about 5ft. long. On one face a shafted cross.

(84) III. (CUMMING, Fig. 32.) A fragment now supposed to be lost. One face with cross pateé in circle, below knot-work, below a man on horseback.

Fig. 3.
THE BOUND LOKI, ANDREAS (5).

RUNIC INSCRIPTIONS.

VARIOUS renderings of our Runic Inscriptions having at different times been published, it will be serviceable to have these brought together in a handy form for reference and comparison. It is unnecessary to repeat the earlier readings made before the runes were clearly deciphered or understood, most of which are quite impossible.

The first to read them correctly was Prof. P. A. Munch, who saw copies of the Casts taken by Bally in 1841. His readings of these, with a Plate showing the Runes, were first published in the Transactions of the Société des Antiquaires du Nord—Vols. for 1845-49. This was published as a separate work by the University of Christiania in 1860. The quotations here given are taken from the latest form in which they appeared as finally revised by his hand, viz., "The Author's Preface" to the "Chronicle of Man and the Sudreys," as published by the Manx Society, Vol. xxii., 1874.

In 1841 W. Kinnebrook published his "Etchings of the Runic Monuments in the Isle of Man." The Etchings, 26, are fairly accurate, but on too small a scale; the inscriptions, however, are hopelessly bad.

Dr. Daniel Wilson, in the Archæology and Prehistoric Annals of Scotland, 1851, gives six of our inscriptions, acknowledging "the assistance of Prof. P. A. Munch in translating them." Probably they were taken from the copies of the Casts at Edinburgh.

In 1852 was published "An Account of the Danes and Norwegians in England, Scotland, and Ireland," by J. J. A. Worsaæ. This work refers to the Crosses in Man, of which Worsaæ had seen the Casts at Edinburgh, and at Canons Ashby. Figures are given of five which have Inscriptions.

The Rev. J. G. Cumming, in 1857, published his "Runic and other Monumental Remains of the Isle of Man," illustrated by Figures taken from photographs of Casts,

which, by the assistance of Sir Henry Dryden, of Canons
Ashby, he was enabled to have made. Where the Inscriptions, as shown in Runes on his lithographed figures,
differ from his letter-press, is here pointed out. Some of
these Casts (of which unfortunately the moulds are now
fallen to pieces) still remain, and are preserved in a
room at Castle Rushen; in all, there are twenty-five
pieces, more or less perfect, including eleven Inscriptions. On the back of one which is broken, the
writer has found the name of the Italian engaged to
take the Casts, together with the date, viz., "L. Canepa,
12th May, 1853. *Viva l'Italia e la liberta; morte a le Tiranni
della patria*," a pious wish realized when, eight years later,
the first Italian Parliament met at Turin. As the Casts do
not always tally with Cumming's translitterations, readings are here added of those which still remain, which
have been carefully examined and transcribed for this
purpose. An earlier set of Casts was taken by W. Bally
in 1841, for a Mr Jones, of Manchester, and these, eleven
in all, are in the possession of Sir Henry Dryden. For
the most part they are of the same Inscriptions as those in
Castle Rushen. Mr Cumming subsequently, in 1868,
contributed an essay on "The Runic Inscriptions of the
Isle of Man," to the Manx Society, Vol. xv. As the
renderings, and especially the translations there given
frequently differ from his former readings, and some new
Inscriptions are added, these also are here quoted or
referred to in each instance. This Essay is accompanied
by a Plate giving the Inscriptions in Runic Characters,
and where discrepancies exist between the Plate and the
letter-press, they are pointed out.

Mr William Kneale, of Douglas, in 1860, brought out a
Guide to the Isle of Man. Since the first edition of this
Catalogue was published, a copy of this little work (long
out of print) was kindly lent to the writer, from which he
has been able to revise the quotations.

The latest authority on the subject is Dr. Vigfusson, of
Oxford, who contributed an article, "The Manx Runic
Inscriptions Re-read," to the "Manx Note Book," No. 9,
January, 1887, from which the readings and translations
here given under his name are taken. These are the more
important since, to quote his own words, "Every reading
given above is the result of careful, and in some cases re-

peated, examination of the Inscriptions on the spot, between the 30th September and the 6th October, 1886." In the Academy [Feby. 26, 1887 No. 773], the writer pointed out some errors into which Dr. Vigfusson's somewhat hurried visit had appeared to lead him, and, at the same time, Canon Isaac Taylor showed from Bally's Casts taken in 1841, and "Squeezes" taken by Sir Henry Dryden, that many of his readings were erroneous. Since the first edition of this little work appeared, we greatly regret to have lost this learned scholar, and it is but justice to his memory to record that, upon paying a second visit to the Island expressly to examine the Inscriptions again, he called upon the writer to acknowledge that in some instances he had fallen into error. Together we visited Andreas and Bride, and when we parted, it was in the full hope of further friendly meetings.

Since the last edition also, namely, in the summer of 1890, G. F. Browne, Disney Professor of Archæology, visited the Island and made a careful examination of the Crosses for the purpose of his series of lectures delivered in Cambridge, with a copy of the Plate of Illustrations of which he has favoured the Author.

In the following pages the writer has given first what he himself believes to be the proper renderings of the Inscriptions, and each of these is followed in order of date by the different readings, if any, given by others. The originals, though in many instances sadly injured, are still in existence, and anyone able to read Runes, may satisfy himself as to which is correct. The figures in brackets appended to the Inscriptions, refer to the foregoing Catalogue, by reference to which the slabs may be more easily identified.

Up to the present, the Author has met with 24 Runic Inscriptions. One is so fragmentary that but a trace of four runes remains; another in Bind-runes (Fig. 1) has not yet been deciphered; the rest are here set down. Unfortunately their epitaphic nature and brief simplicity reduce their historic interest, as they contain no certain reference to any political event, nor throw any light on other records. It is notable that the sculptors' names which appear are all Norse, viz., Gaut, the son of Biarn, Onon, *i.e.* Anund (?), Osruth, Thorbjörn, and Thurith. The other names are for the most part such as were

common at the period, and give no clue to the individu-
ality of the persons. Out of a total of forty-four names
(leaving out the name "Jesu Christ") thirty-two are those
of men, eight of women, and four are nicknames. Of man's
names nineteen are Norse, nine Celtic, three doubtful,
and one Pictish. Of woman's names six are Norse. two
Celtic. Two of the nicknames are Norse, and two doubtful.
There are also three Place Names. Doubtless those in
whose memory the Crosses were erected were great chiefs
and distinguished in their day, but who they were or what
they did we shall probably never learn. And now these
handsome monuments erected "to make their memories
for ever live," are many of them almost worn to nothing,
so truly may we say with Spenser——

> "All such vain moniments of earthlie masse,
>   Devoured of Time, in time to nought do passe."

Fig. 4,

Fig. 5,

Fig. 6,

THORWOLD CROSS, ANDREAS (7).

READINGS AND RENDERINGS.

ANDREAS.

(1) I. . . . THANA : AF : UFAIK : FAUTHUR : SIN :
IN : KAUTR : KIRTHI : SUNR : BIARNAR : FRO KULI.
[*A.B. erected*] this [*cross*] *in memory of Ufaik his father, but Gaut the son of Biorn of Cooiley carved it.* Cooiley (alone or in composition) is not an uncommon place-name in the Island.

As shown by Canon Isaac Taylor the Cast taken by W. Bally (1841) bracketing all defective letters, reads :— . . TH[A]NA : [A]F : UFAIC : FAUTHUR : SIN : [E]N : CAUTR : CIRTHI : SUNR : BIARNAR : FRO : CUL[I].

MUNCH.

(Manx Soc. Vol. xxii. p. 28.)—6 . . THANA AF VFAIC FAVTHVR SIN IN CAVTR CIRTHI SVNR BIARNAR CVBCVLI,—
. . . *hanc (sc. crucem) post Ufeigum patrem suum, sed Gautus fecit, filius Björnonis.*

WORSAÆ has the same, omitting the last two words.

CUMMING.

(Runic Remains p. 22)— . . . CRUS : THANA : AF : UFAIG : FAUTHUR : SIN : IN : GAUTR : GUTTHI : SUNR : BIARNAR : (CUB : CULI ?). i.e. *A.B. erected this cross to Ufaig his father, but Gaut Bjornson made it.*

The runes in Fig. 10, Pl. III. correspond with this reading, except that the CR of the first word is omitted and that the ninth word appears as KIRTHI.

(Manx Soc. Vol. xv., p. 26,) Inscription as in Fig. 10. Translation as before, with the further suggestion that the last two words may be an "agnomen of Gaut and signify 'Sealkiller.'" In the Plate—No II.—the runes appear, as before, with CRUS in full; but the ninth word is now spelled KURTHI, and the last eight runes of the inscription are dotted, as being "doubtful."

KNEALE.

In the Plate of Inscriptions, No. 16, gives the same reading as the last, omitting the last two words. This is repeated at p. 164, and translated—*(N.N. erected) this (cross) to his father Ofeig, but Gaut Björnson made it.*

VIGFUSSON.

4——AFTIR : UFAAC : FAUTHUR : SIN : EN : CAUTR : CIRTHI : SAUNR : BIARNAR : FRA : CULI. *(N. raised this cross) to the memory of Ufaac [O'Faac] his father. But Gaut the son of Biorn of Culi worked it.*

(4) II. Inscription in Bind Runes not yet deciphered. See Fig. 1, p. 1.

(6) III. SONT : ULF : HIN : SUARTI : RAISTI : KRUS : THONA : AFTIR : ARIN : BIAURK : KUINU : SINA.
Sandulf the Black erected this cross to the memory of Arinbjörg his wife.

MUNCH.

(Manx Soc. Vol. xxii., p. 28.)—13. SANTULF EIN SVARTI RAISTI KRVS thANA AFTIR ARIN BIAVRC CVINV SINA :— *Sandulfus niger erexit crucem hanc post Arinbjargam uxorem suam.*

WORSAÆ.

SANDULF EIN SVARTI RAISTI KRUS THANA AFTIR ARIN BIAURG KUINU SINA.—*Sandulf the Swarthy erected this cross to his wife Arnbjörg.* The Plate, at p. 282, gives THONA and SINO.

CUMMING.

The Cast in Castle Rushen,—SONT : ULF : HIN : SUARTI : RAISTI : KRUS : THONA : AFTIR : ARINBI[A]URK : KUI[N]U : SIN[A].

(Runic Remains, p. 22.)—SAND : ULF : EINS : SUARTI : RAISTI : KRUS : THONA : AFTIR : ARIN : BIAURK : KUINO : SINO, i.e. *Sandulf the Black erected this cross to his wife Arinbjörg.* The runes figured in Pl. III., Fig. 9, give the same reading.

(Manx Soc. Vol. xv., p. 30.) Inscription as before. The translation also is the same, except that the word "Swarthy" is substituted for "Black."

KNEALE.

SANDULF : EIN : SUARTI : RAISTI : KRUS : THANA : AFTIR : ARIN : BIAURG : KUINU : SINA. In the Plate of Inscriptions, 14, he gives the same, but divides the first word and gives the o rune in THONA and SINO.

VIGFUSSON.

13. SONT : ULF : EIN : SUARTI : RAISTI : CRUS : THONO : AFTER : ARIN : BIAURC : CUNU : SINA. *Sandulf the Black raised this cross to the memory of Arinbiorg his wife.*

(7) IV. THURUALTR : RAISTIKRUS : TH[ON ——. *Thorwold erected this cross [to the memory of A.B., &c.]* See Fig. ,6 p. 33.

VIGFUSSON.

12. THURUALTR : RAISTI : CRUS : THO——. *Thorwold raised this cross —— ——*

(8) V. ——RAISTI : KRUS : THAANA , AFTIR . . . [A.B.] *erected this cross to the memory of [C.D.] &c.*

BALLAUGH.

(9) I. OULAIBR : LIUTULBSUNR : RAISTI : KRS: THANA : AIFTIR : U[L]B : SUN. SIN. *Olave the son of Liutwolf raised this cross to the memory of [Wolf?] his son.*

MUNCH.

(Manx Society, Vol. xxii, p. 27.) 3. THORLIBR THIVTVLB SVNR RAIST CRVS thaNA AIFTIR VB SVN SIN. *Thorleifus Thjodulfi (Thiostulfi) filius erexit crucem hanc post Ubbonem (Ulfum) filium suum.* (The Plate gives the runes AIBR as the ending of the first word.)

CUMMING.

Cast —OULAIBR ⦂ [L]IUTULB. SUNR ⦂ [RAISTI ⦂ K]RS. TH[A]NA AIFTIR ⦂ U[L]B ⦂ SUN. SIN.

Canon Taylor takes the first name to be THURLAIB[I]R, and the next to begin with TH not L. He also reads R[A]STI ⦂ CRUS ⦂ TH[]N[A] ⦂ AFT ⦂ F.

(Runic Remains, p. 17.) THORLAIBR ⦂ THORIULB ⦂ SUNR ⦂ RAISTI ⦂ CRS ⦂ THONA ⦂ AIFTIR ⦂ ULB ⦂ SUN ⦂ SIN ⦂ i.e., *Thorlaf the son of Thorjôlf erected this cross to Olave his son.* The runes are given in accordance with this reading in the Plate—I. Fig. 2a.

(Manx Society, Vol. xv., p. 30.) The above reading is repeated ; and in the Plate, No. X, the runes are the same, except that THANA stands for THONA, and the eighth word is in dotted letters, the last rune of all being also dotted.

KNEALE.

In the Plate 13. THORLAIBR ⦂ THORIULB ⦂ SUNR ⦂ RAISTI ⦂ KRUS ⦂ THONA ⦂ AIFTIR ⦂ ULB ⦂ SUN ⦂ SIN; but in the body of the Guide, p. 167, this is given :—THARLIBR THARIULB SUNR RAISTI KRUS THANA AFTIR ULB SUN SIN, i.e., *Thorlaf Thorjolfson erected this cross to his son Ulf.*

VIGFUSSON.

6. OULAIBR ⦂ LIUTULBSUNR ⦂ RA— —US ⦂ THONA ⦂ AFTIR ⦂ ULBSUNSIN. *Aulaib [i.e., Olaf] the son of Liutwolf [i.e., Leod-wolf] ra[ised] this [cr]oss to the memory of Wolf his son.*

BRADDAN.

(12) I. X[TH..]FEAAK ⦂ RAISTI ⦂ KRUS ⦂ THANO ⦂ IFT ⦂ UFAAK ⦂ SUN ⦂ KRINAAS.

X[*Th..*]*feaac erected this cross to the memory of Ufaac the son of Crinaa.*

CUMMING.

(Manx Soc. Vol. xv., p. 31.)—THURKETIL : RAISTI : CRUS : THANO : AFT : UFAIG : SUN : KLINAIS. *Thorketil erected this cross to Ufaig Klinaison.* The Plate (XI) gives the runes of above reading, but the first word in dotted letters.

KNEALE.

In his Guide, p. 45, THURSTEIN RAISTA KRUS THANN EFT UFAAG SUN KLINAIS. *Thorstein erected this cross to Ofeig Klinaisön.* And at p. 94, THUR......RAISTI KRUS THANN, &c., as above, adding "The last five runes in the first name have been almost obliterated and are illegible."

VIGFUSSON.

5, [MA]LFIAAC : RAISTI : CRUS : THANA : IFT : UFAAC : SUN : CRINAAS. *(Ma)lfiaac raised this cross to the memory of Ufaac [i.e. O'Faac] the son of Crinaa.*

Prof. G. F. BROWNE reads the first word ULFEAAK, and and the last KRINAIS. The first name however is certainly neither *Ulfeaak* nor *Malfiaac*, the first two runes are perfectly distinct and certainly THU ; the next is broken, but is a possible R. Whether such a name as THURFEAAK be known the Author cannot say, but can make nothing else of this.

(13) II. . . [N or H?] ROSKITIL : UILTI : I : TRIKU : AITHSOARA : SIIN.

. . *Hvossketil betrayed in a truce his (fellow) oath-swearer.* The first part of the Inscription runs up the shaft of the cross, the last two words in another line, above the words I : TRIKU.

MUNCH.

(Manx Soc. Vol. xxii., p. 28.)—12 . . . . R ASKITIL VILTI I TRICV AITHSQARA SIIN. *Quem Ascatillus decepit in treuga consacramentalem suum.*

WILSON gives this, p. 540, OSKITIL UILTI I TRIGU AITHSUARA SINN. *Oskitil betrayed in truce his sworn friend.* And WORSAÆ p. 283, the same, but the first word with an A and the next to the last SAARA, translating— *Whom Asketil deceived in security, contrary to his pledge of peace.*

D

CUMMING.

Cast—[N ?]ROSKITIL : UILTI : I : TRIKU : AITHSOARA : SIIN.
CANON TAYLOR thinks the first letter must certainly
have been H. The last word SINA or SINO.

(Runic Remains, p. 24.)— . . R : OSCITIL : VII.TI : I :
TRIGU : AITH : SOARA : SIIN. *Whom Osketel deceived
under the security of his pledge of peace.* The runes for
above reading are given in Plate III., Fig. 12 b.

(Manx Soc. Vol. xv. p. 31.)—ER : OSKETIL : VILDI : I :
DRIKU : AITH : SOARA : SIIN. *Here Osketel bewailed in a
drinking feast Aitha his mother-in-law.* The Plate gives
in runes, No. XII., . . [O]R : OSKITIL : and the
remaining runes as above.

KNEALE.

Plate of Inscriptions, 3, OSKITIL : RISTI : I : TRIKU :
AITHSOARA : SIIN. At p. 94 of the Guide—ASKITIL
VILTI I TRIGU AITHSAARA SIIN, i.e., *Whom Asketil
deceived in security, contrary to his pledge of peace.*

VIGFUSSON.

20 . . . N : ROSCIL : UILTI : I : TRICV [M] : AITHSOARA :
SIN. *(But) Horsecel betrayed his oath-fellow under his faith.*

(16) III. UTR : RISTI : KRUS : THONO : AFT : FROKA
[F]ATH [UR : SIN : IN : THU. . |
Odd erected this cross to Froca his [father, but Thor . .]

MUNCH.

(Manx Society, Vol. xxii, p. 27.) 4, VTR RISTI CRVS
THANA AFT FRACA FATHVR SIN THVRBIAVRN . . . *Ottarus
(Gautus) erexit crucem hanc post Franconum patrem suum,
sed Thorbjornus* . . . (The Plate shows the word IN
between the last two words.)

CUMMING.

(Runic Remains, p. 31.)—As above, with the addition
of the following—THU)RBIAURN : SUNR : (N. N.
GIRTHI) i.e , *Ottar erected this Cross to Froga, his Father,
but Thorbjorn son of (N. N. made it.)* In the Plate
VIII., Fig. 23, the runes read as in the letter-
press.

(Manx Soc. Vol. xv., p. 26.) The same reading and rendering as above, and in the Plate (III) the runes for the same are given, but the last word in dotted letters.

KNEALE.

Plate, 2—UTR : RISTI : KRUS : THONO : AFT : FROKA : FATHURSIN : IN : THURBIAURN : SUNR. At p. 93 of the Guide this is given—UTR RISTI KRUS THANA AFT FRAKA FATHUR SIN IN THURBIAURN SUNK, i.e., *Ottar erected this cross to his father Frakka, but Thorbjörn the son (of N. N. made it)*.

VIGFUSSON.

17, UTR : RISTI : CRUS : THONO : AFT : FROCA — —. *Odd raised this cross to the memory of Froca.*

(17) IV. THURLABR : NEAKI : RISTI : KRUS : THONO : AFT : FIAK : SUN : SIN : BRUTHUR : SUN : EABRS×

Thorlaf Neaci, Brother's son to Eab, raised this cross to the memory of Fiac his son.

MUNCH.

(Manx Society, Vol. xxii., p. 29.) 16. THVRLABR NEACI RISTI CRVS THANA AFT FIAK SVN IN BRVTHVR SVN IABRS. *Thorlavus Neaki erexit crucem hanc post Fiac filium (suum) sed fratris filium Jabri* The plate gives THONO as the spelling of the fifth word.

WILSON, p. 542, gives the same reading, but I for A in the first word, and bracketing S and B in the eighth and tenth.

WORSAÆ also, p. 281, gives the same, but omits SVN IN. He translates—*Thorlaf Neaki erected this cross to Fiak . . brother, a son of Jabr.*

CUMMING.

Cast—THURL[A]BR : NEAKI ; RISTI : KRUS : THONO : AFT : FIAK : S[. . . . . . .] : BRUTHUR : SUN : EABRS.

(Runic Remains, p. 29.) As above. *Thorlaf Neaki erected this cross to Fiak his son, brother's son to Jabr.* The runes—Plate VIII., Fig. 22, give the same reading.

(Manx Society, Vol. xv., p. 27.) The same reading, but FIAK is spelled with an E for I. The same reading is given in runes, Plate No. IV. In the translation the seventh word is spelled *Feake*, and the last word *Jaf*.

KNEALE.

Plate, I. THURLABR : NEAKI : RISTI : KRUS : THONO : AFT : FIAK ; SUN : SIN : BRUTHUR : SUN : EABRS. At p. 92, he translates,—*Thorlaf Neaki erected this cross to Fiach his son, the nephew (brother's son) of Eabr.*

VIGFUSSON.

16. THURLIBR : NEACI : RISTI : CRUS : THONO : AFT : FIAK : SUN : SIN : BRUTHUR : SUN : EABS. *Thorlaf Neaci, brother's son to Eab, raised this cross to the memory of Fiak, his son.*

(18) V. THURBIAURN : RISTI : KRUS : TH— —
Thorbjörn erected this cross [to the memory of C.D., &c.]

VIGFUSSON.

15. THURBIAURN : RISTI : KRUS : THON — —. *Thorbjörn raised this cross——*

BRIDE.

(21) I. TRUIAN : SURTUFKALS : RAISTI ; KRSTHINA : AF[K]ATHMIU[L] : KUNU : SINA : i.e.,
Druian, the son of Dugald, raised this cross to the memory of [K]athmaoil his wife.

Near the village of Bride is a Quarterland which still bears the name of Glion Truan.

VIGFUSSON.

2 TRUIAN : SUR : TUFKALS : RAISTI : CR : THINA : AFCATHMIUL CUNU : SIN [A] .—*Druian the son of Dufgal raised this cross to the memory of Cathmaoil his wife.*

CONCHAN.

(26) I. (. . . bruthu)R SUNR × RAISTI × AFTI ×
　　　UINI [A]SINA
　　MURKIALU × M. . . .
　　× UKIKAT × AUKRATHIFRIT
　　. . A × NI . .

On the other face of the slab, the words—

　　× KRU [S]
　　× ISUKRIST
　　THURITH × RAIST × RUNER. . .

　　*(A.B., C.D's. . . . brothe)r's son × raised (this) to the
　　　　memory of his friends*
　　Murkialu M. . . .
　　Ugigat × and Rathfrid . .
　　× *The Cross*
　　× *Jesus Christ*
　　Thurith × carved × (these) runes

MUNCH.

(Manx Soc. Vol. xxii., p. 29.) 17, CRVS—*crucem.* ISVCRIST
—*Jesu Krist.* THURITH RAIST RVNAR—*Thurida sculpsit
literas.* SVNR RAISTI AFTIR SVN SINA MVRKIBLV.—Tak-
ing SVN to be a mis-spelling for CUNV and the B in the
last word for A, he thus translates this portion :—
. . *filius erexit (crucem) post uxorem suam Muriellam.*
VCICAT ASVIK ATHICRIT AM . . . NTH—un-
translated.

CUMMING.

Cast— . KRU [S] . ISUKRIST.
On the other face, [R]AISTI . [A]FTI [UINIA] SINA
MURKI [A]LU RATHI [K]RIT. The rest being broken
off.

(Runic Remains, p. 33.) CRU ISUCHRIST THURITH RAIST :
RUNER . . . SUNR : RAISTI : AFTIR : SUN : SINA :
MURKIBLU UGIGAT : ASUIR : ATHIGRIT AM : I
*Cross. Jesus Christ. Thurith engraved (or made) the
runes. (N.N's) son erected this to his son . Murkiblu.* In
the Plate X., Fig. 26, the runes are given for the
above reading.

(Manx Soc. Vol. xv., p. 28.) The same reading, but a totally different and quite impossible translation, namely—" . . *am I . . . (lies buried) over agains our Athigrit (N.N's) son erected (this) to his son in mourning* The rest of the legend is given as before. In the Plate (VII.) the Runes are given as before.

KNEALE.

In Plate 17. KRUS . . SUNR ✕ RAISTI ✕ IFT ✕ KUINUSINA ✕ MURKIALU ✕ M . . ✕ UKIKAT ✕ AUKR ✕ ATHIKRIT ✕ IN ✕ K . . THURITH ✕ RAIST ✕ RUNER . . ISUKRIST.

In the body of the Guide, p. 109—KRUS . . . SUNR RAISTI EFT KUINU SINA MYRGIALU M . . . UGIGAD AUKR ATHIGRID . . . THURITH RAIST RUNER . . . . ISU KRIST, i e., [A.B.] *son of [C.D.,] erected [this] cross to Mirgiol his wife, mother of Hugigud, Haukr, [and] Athigrid. Thurid engraved [these] Runes . . . Jesus Christ.*

VIGFUSSON.

18 — — SUNR ✕ RAISTI ✕ IFT [3 letters] LUSINA —*the son raised this after his?*
MURCIOLU ✕ M[OTHUR . SINA]
✕ UCIFAT . AUKRATHICR ✕ T . . . . *and of wise counsel* (auk rathigr) . IESUCRIST CRIST THURITH RAIST RUNIR. *Thurith carved the runes.*

CANON TAYLOR points out that CRIST is plainly CRUS; and Cumming's reading, *aftir sun sin* agrees better with the Cast than Vigfusson's *ift . . . lusina,* of which he makes no sense. The reading *aucraither,* he thinks impossible.

GERMAN.

(34) I. INOSRU[TH]R : RAIST : RUNAR : THSAR ✕ — — *He Osruth carved these runes.*

MUNCH.

(Manx Soc. Vol. xxii., p. 29.)—14 . . INAIRVIR RAIST RVNAR THAER AFTIR . . *(ineirvir?) sculpsit literas hasce post.*

CUMMING.

(Runic Remains, p. 19.) INOSRUIR : RAIST : RUNAR : THENR AFTIR . . . *Inosruir carved these runes to — —*. The proper runes for this reading, omitting the first and the last letters, are given in Plate II., Fig. 5.

(Manx Society, Vol. xv., p. 37.) Same reading as above, but in the fourth word an s instead of N. In the Plate (VI.), the runes are given as above, but the last five runes of the first word, the A of RUNAR, and the last four runes of AFTIR, in dots.

KNEALE.

5, INOS RUIR : RAIST RUNAR THSNR.—In the body of the Guide, p. 181, this is given.—INA SVRTR RAIST RUNAR THSER, i.e., *Ina the swarthy engraved these runes.*

VIGFUSSON.

19, INOSRUTHR : RAIST : RUNAR : THSAR × *But Osruth carved these runes.*

(36) II. . . . US. THENSI. IFTER. ASRITHI. KUNUSINO. [T]U[T]URUT. . . . R. A. . . .
[*A.B. raised this cr*]*oss to the memory of Asrith his wife* [*daughter of — —*]

CUMMING.

(Runic Remains, p. 33.) . . US. THENSI. EFTER. ASRITHI. KUNU SINA : DUTUR : UT. . . RAIST. . . i.e. *A.B. erected this cr)oss to Asrith his wife: the daughter of Ut* [r] *'Oter ?*)—*C.D. carved these runes.*

Manx Soc. Vol. xv., p. 32.) Same as above, but I instead of E in IFTIR. In the Plate (XVI.) the runes are the same but the R of KRUS is given, and the word TUTVR as well as the 3rd and 4th runes of the last word are dotted, as though doubtful or not clear.

KNEALE.

Plate 6.—US : THENI : EFTIR : ASRITHI : KUNU : SINA : TUTUR : UTR— And, at p. 171, US THENA EFTIR ASRITHI KUNU SINA DUTUR UTR—i.e. (*N.N. erected*) *this cross to his wife Asrid, daughter of Ottar.*

VIGFUSSON.

> 14.—US · THENEI · IFTER · ASRITHI · CUNU · SINO (4 strokes) URU · T— — (*N. raised*) *this* (*cr*)*oss to the memory of Asrith his wife*— —

JURBY.

(40) I....UN : SIN : IN : ONON : RAITI, .e.,

> . . . . *his son but Onon writ...*

MUNCH.

> (Manx Soc. Vol. xxii., p. 29.) 15 ...RV SVN IN aNAN RAITI FAIRTHUR IAL... ...*ræ filium sed aliam* (*crucem*) *erexit Fairthurus Jal...*

CUMMING.

> Cast—[. . UN . . . .]N : ONON : RAITI : . . . FAIRTHUR : [BR...]

> (Runic Remains, p. 23.) ... RU : SUN : IN : ONON : RASTI : AFT : FAITHUR : BR...... ...*Ro's son but Onon erected it to his father's brother.* Plate III., Fig. 11, gives the runes for the same reading, but the sixth word is not clear.

> (Manx Society, vol. xv., p. 30.) Same reading as before, but an I instead of S in RAITI, and the last rune is followed by U. Translation as above. In the Plate (VIII) the runes read the same, except that the seventh word is spelled FAIRTHUR; the first rune R, and the last two RU, are dotted.

KNEALE.

> 12. RU : SUN : IN : ONON : RAISTI : AFT : FAUTHUR : BR...
> In the body of the Guide (p. 167) this is given—
> ...RU SUN IN ANAN RAITI AFT FAIRTHUR BR... i.e. ...*ru's son, but Annan erected it to* (*his*) *father's brother...*

VIGFUSSON.

> 11. —N : AN : ONON : RAITI : — — *N. But Onon wrote—*,

MAUGHOLD.

(58) II.   [HIR LI]KI[A I]N KRISTH : MALAKI : OK
BATHRIC : ATHANMAN : UNAL . SAUTHAR : IUAN
ARIST : IKURNATHAL.

*[Here lie i]n Christ Malachi and Patrick Adamnan Unal (O'Neill)
Sheep-John carved (these runes) in Kurna Dale.*

(70) I.   A fragment has been found in this parish showing
traces of an Inscription, too broken however to decipher.
It is to be hoped the rest of the cross may yet be found.

MICHAEL.

(71) I. · . . .   [KRU]S : THNA : AFT[IR]   .   .

[A.B. erected] this cross in memory of [C.D.]

MUNCH.

(Manx Soc., Vol. xxii., p. 28.)   (7) ...CRVS THAN AFTIR...
"In t h a n the final 'a' is omitted because the next
word begins with an 'a.'   *Crucem hanc post.*

CUMMING.

Cast—[KRU]S : THNA : AF[TIR]

(Runic Remains, p. 19.)   . . . CRUS : THNA : AFTIR : i.e ,
This cross to, "the names having altogether disap-
peared."   In Plate II, Fig. 4, the runes give above
reading,—the top of the last R broken off.

(Manx Society, Vol. xv, p. 32.)   Same reading and
translation ; and the plate, xv, gives the runes as above.

KNEALE.

4   KRUS : THAN : AFTIR.

VIGFUSSON.

10   CRUS : THAN : AFTIR.

(72) II. × MAIL : BRIKTI : SUNR : ATHAKANS : SMITH :
RAISTI : KRUS : THANO : FUR : SALU : SINA : SIN :
BRUKUIN : KAUT ×   Then on the face of the Cross, on the
space to the right above the circle, KIRTHI : THANO : AUK
terminating on the corresponding space to the left of the head
of the Cross, ALA : I MAUN ×

*Mal Brigd, son of Athakan, smith, raised this cross for his soul, his
tenant Gaut carved this and all in Man.*

MUNCH.

(Manx Soc., Vol. xxii., p. 27.)—5. MAIL BRICTI SVNR ATHACANS SMITH RAISTI CRVS THANA FVR SALV SINA SIN BRVCVIN CAVT CIRTHI THANa AVC ALA IMAVN. *Mael-brigidus filius Athacani fabri erexit crucem hanc pro anima sua (peccatrice) Gautus fecit hanc (sc. crucem) et omnes in Mannia.*

WILSON, at p. 539, gives in his figure the runes as read by Munch, but SINI for SINA, and KAUT[s] for KAUT. He translates—*Mailbrikti, son of Athacan, the smith, raised this cross for his soul, and that of his faithful friend Gaut, who made this [cross] and all [the crosses] in Man.*

WORSAÆ, p. 284, also follows Munch, but gives SINI, THANA, and MANN, which, however, in the figure appear as SINA, THANO, and MAUN. His translation is the same, omitting the word BRUKUIN, as Munch had done.

CUMMING.

(Runic Remains, p. 16.) MAIL : BRIGDI : SUNR : ATHAKANS : SMITH : RAISTI : CRUS : THANO : FUR : SALU : SINI : SIN : BRUKUIN : GAUT : GIRTHI : THANO : AUK : ALA : I MAUN ; i.e. *Malbrigd, the son of Athakan the smith, erected this (cross) for his soul, but his kinsman (?) Gaut made this and all in Man.*

The runes for same reading are given in the Plate I, Fig. 1.

(Manx Soc. Vol. xv., p. 22.)—Same reading as above, but ᴧUK : ALA written as one word,—AUGALA. The translation greatly differs, viz.:—*Mailbrigd, the son of Athakan, as a work of art, erected this cross for his soul. His betrothed (or bride) made (or caused) Gaut to chisel it in Man.* The Plate, I, gives the runes as in "Runic Remains."

KNEALE.

11. MAIL : BRIKTI : SUNR : ATHAKANS : SMITH : RAISTI KRUS : THANO : FUR : SILU : SANA : SIN : BRUKUIN : KAUT : KIRTHI : THANO : AUK : ALA : IMAVN—At p. 183 he gives the same reading, but A for O in THANO, and SALU SINA for SILU SANA. His translation is the same as WORSAÆ's.

VIGFUSSON.

3. MAL : BRICTI : SUNR : ATHAKANS : SMITH : RAISTI :
CRUS : THANO : FUR : SALU : SINA : SIN : BRUKUIN
GOUT : CIRTHI : THANO : AUC : ALA : IMAUN. *Malbricti
the Smith, son of Athacan, raised this cross for his own soul.
His surety-friend Gout worked this (cross) and all in Mann.*

CANON TAYLOR reads MAIL or MAEL, THONO, and GAUT on
the Cast.

(73) III. *(a)* MAL : LUMKUN : RAISTI : KRUS : THENA :
EFTER : MAL . MURU : FUSTRA : SINE : TOTIR :
TUFKALS KONA : [A]S : ATHISL : ATI.
*Mal-Lumkun raised this cross to the memory of Mal-muru his foster
[·daughter?] the daughter of Dugald, whom Athisl had (to wife).*

(b) ETRA : ES : LAIFA : FUSTRA : KUTHAN : THAN :
SON : ILAN.
Better is it to leave a good foster than a bad son.

MUNCH.

(Manx Soc., Vol. xxii., p. 26.) *a.* 1. MAL LVMCVN
RAISTI CRVS THANA EFTER MAL MVRV FVSTRA SINA
TOTER TVFCALS OS ATHISL ATI. *Mallumsun erexit crucem
hanc post Malmuram educatricem suam, filiam Dugaldi,
quam Adislus habuit (i.e., in matrimonio).* The Plate
shows the word KONA between TUFKALS and OS.

b. 2. ...ITRA ES LAIFA FVSTRA CVTHAN SVN ILAN.
"Of 'itra es' nothing satisfactory can be made out.
...L e i f a, acc. form of L e i t i, seems to be the
name of the person or one of the persons in question."
Of the remaining four words Prof. Munch says—
"*educatorem, bonum, filium malum,* curious words, showing
that these inscriptions were not only panegyrics.
Whether, however, both epithets refer to one person
or to two, is impossible to say, as we have not the
whole.

WILSON, p. 541. *Mallymcun raised this cross after Malmor
his foster son.*

WORSAÆ, p. 283. *Mal Lumkun erected this cross to his foster
father, Malmor.*

CUMMING.

All that can now be read on the Cast at Castle Rushen is A : EFTIR : MAL : MURU : FUSTRA : SI[NE] : TOTIR : TUFKALS : KONA : [ ] S : ATHISL : ATI. The other legend does not appear to have been taken by Canepa.

(Runic Remains, p. 34.) *a.* NIAL : LUMKUN : RAISTI : CRUS : THANA : EFTIR : MAL : MURU : FUSTRA : SINA : DOTIR : DUFGALS : KONA : OS : ATHISI : ATI ; i.e., *Niel Lumkun raised this cross to Maelmor his foster-mother, daughter of Dugald the keen, whom Athisi had (to wife).*

b. ...TRA : ES : LAIFA : FUSTRA : GUTHAN : THAN SON : ILAN ...... This, which Cumming supposed to be another inscription on a separate stone, is not translated. The Runes shown in Plate XI, Figs. 28b and 29, are in accordance with the letterpress, but in "*a*" the next to the last word has a T for TH.

(Manx Society, Vol. xv., p. 33.) *a.* Same as in Runic Remains, translating—*Niel Lumgun erected this cross to Maelmore his foster-child, the daughter of Dugald, whose wife (widow) Athisi he possessed.*

b. (p. 35.) The first word begins with s,—STRA ; otherwise as before. He adds Mr. Carr's rendering, than which he "can conjecture no better": *to foster-father Isleif, the good foster-father, towards an evil son.* In the Plate, XVII. and XVIII., the runes read as in "Runic Remains," but, in the tenth word s, I, and A are dotted, and in the following word T and O. The other part of the Inscription (*b*) begins with s dotted,

KNEALE.

Plate, 8—MAL : LUMCUN : RAISTI : KRUS : THANA : EFTIR : MAL : MURU : FUSTRA SINA : TOTIR : TUFKALS : KONA : IS : ATHISI : ATI; and, 15—TRA : ES : LAIFA : FUSTRA : KUTHAN : SUN : ILAN. At p. 184 this is given: *Mal Lumkun erected this cross to Malmora his foster-mother, daughter of Dugald the Keen (or clever) whom Athisi had to wife.*

VIGFUSSON.

I. MAL : LUMCUN : RISTI : CRUS : THENA : EFTER : MAL-MURU : FOSTRA : SINA : TOTER : TUFCALS : CONO :

ES : ATHISL : ATTI. *Mal-Lumcun [i.e. Mael-Lomchon] raised this cross to the memory of Mal-Muru his foster-mother, daughter of Dufgal, the woman whom Athisl had to wife.*

The motto is :—[BE] TRA : ES : LAIFA : FUSTRA : CUTHAN : THAN : SON : ILAN. *Better it is to leave a good foster than a bad son.*

CANON TAYLOR reads *raisti, fustra, totir, cona,* and *ati. Mal* instead of *Nial* he thinks undoubtedly correct.

(74) IV. KRIM : RISTI : KRUS : THNA : AFT : RUMUN...... IN. i.e.
Grim erected this cross to the memory of Hromund his— —.

MUNCH.

(Manx Soc. Vol. xxii., p. 28.)—9. . . . SVAC RAISTI CRUS THAN EFT RVMVN . . . NT.—*Svangus erexit crucem hanc post Romondum.* . .

CUMMING.

Cast :—SUAK : RISTI : KRUS : THNA : [A]FT : RUMUN. . . The Cast certainly has the first word as here given.

(Runic Remains, p. 18).—SUAK : RISTI : CRUS : THNA : EFT : RUMUN . . NT. *Suag erected this cross to Römön.* The runes in Plate II, Fig. 3, correspond.

Manx Soc. Vol. xv., p. 32.)—SVIG, &c , as above. The runes in the Plate, XIV, are in accordance with this reading, the last two letters of the first word dotted.

KNEALE.

9. KRIM RISTI : KRUS : THAN : EFT : RUMUN—*Grim erected this cross to Hromund.*

VIGFUSSON.

9. [GRIMR : IN : SUA]RTI : RISTI : CRUS : THAN : AFT : RUMU[13 letters]IN. He has "little doubt" the legend ended,—RUMU[ND : BRUTHUR . SUN : S]IN. "As different readings have been given of the beginning of the existing part of the legend, and the runes are a little damaged, it is better to add that there is no doubt that RTI is the proper reading."

(75) V.✕IUALFIR : SUNR ; THURULFS : HINS : RAUTHA :
RISTI : KRUS : THONO : AFT : FRITHU : MUTHUR :
SINO. ✕

*Joalf, son of Thorolf the Red, raised this cross to the memory of Fritha
his mother.*

MUNCH.

(Manx Soc., Vol. xxii., p. 28.)—10. IVALFIR SVNR
THVRVLFS EINS RAVTHA RISTI CRVS THANA AFT FRITHV
MVTHVR SINa—*Joalfus filius Thorulfi rufi erexit crucem
hanc post Fridam matrem suam.*

So WORSAÆ, p. 282.

CUMMING.

Cast :—[JUALFI]R : [S]UNR : TH[U]RU[LFS] : HINS :
RAUTHA : RISTI : KRUS : THONO : AFT : FRITHU : MUTHUR :
SIN[O].

(Runic Remains, p. 24.)—JUALFR : RUNR : THURULFS :
EINS : RAUTHA : RISTI : CRUS : THONO : AFT : FRITHU :
MUTHUR : SINA i.e. *Joalf the son of Thorolf the Red,
erected this cross to his mother Frida.* The runes as
given in Plate IV., Fig. 13d, correspond with this
reading, save that there is an I before the R in
Jualfir, and the last word ends in o not A.

(Manx Soc., Vol. xv., p. 27.)—Exactly the same as in
letter-press of " Runic Remains." The runes in the
Plate, V., correspond, but again the I appears in
Jualfir.

KNEALE.

(7) IUALFIR : SUNR : THURULFS : EINS : RAUTHA : RISTI :
KRUS : THONO : AFT : FRITHU : MUTHUR : SINO—. Translated at p. 187. *Joalf, son of Thorolf the Red, erected this
cross to his mother Frida.*

VIGFUSSON.

(7) AULAFIR : SUNR : THURULFS : EINS : RAUTHA : RISTI :
CRUS : THANA : AFT : FRITHU : MOTHUR : SINA. *Olaf,
the son of Thorwolf the Red, raised this cross to the memory
of Fritha his mother.*

(76) VI. . . . KRIMS : INS : SUARTI. i.e.
|*A.B. erected this cross to the memory of C.D.———? of Grim the
Black.*

MUNCH.

(Manx Soc., Vol. xxii., p. 28.)—(7 and 8) . . . CRIMS INS SVARTA . . . *Grimi nigri.*

CUMMING.

Cast :— KRIMS : INS : SUARTA.

(Runic Remains, p. 21.)— GRIMS : INS : SUARTA; *Grims the Black.* Plate II., Fig. 8c., the runes are given the same reading.

(Manx Soc., Vol. xv., p. 32.)—Same as above, but the last word ends in I not A. The runes in the Plate, XIII., correspond.

KNEALE.

10. KRIMS : IN : SUARTA. At p. 187, EINS for INS— *Grim the Swarthy.*

VIGFUSSON.

8— —RIMS : INS : SUARTA. (*N. raised this cross to the memory of M. his mother [or wife] (daughter) of (G)rim the Black.*

———

NOTE.—In MUNCH's transliterations the small "a" always represents the Manks rune for "o."

LATIN INSCRIPTION.

————

ONE very interesting Inscription has been found in Roman Uncials. This is on a rough piece of whin stone, now in Government Office, which is "said to have been dug up 6ft. from under ground when the present Church was being built" at Santon. It measures 3ft. 6in. by 9in., and 4½in. thick. The Inscription is clearly cut on a space, about 22in. long, slightly sunk and smoothed, and reads,

AVIT ⊢ MONO
MENT ⊢

(The place) of the tomb of Avitus.

Huëbner's " Inscriptiones Brittaniæ Christianæ" gives MORO MERTI for the second word.

It is figured by Cumming, 48, who quotes Oswald's and Jamieson's accounts from the Transactions of the Society of Antiquaries, Vol. II., Pt. 2.

Dr. Jamieson thought the characters pretty nearly resembled "the old Teutonic as given by Astle, Tab. I., p. 64. The initial M in 'Monomentum' has the precise form of that of the specimen of Roman Uncials, which he gives from a most ancient copy of the four Gospels preserved in the Harleian Library (vide Tab. xi., p. 84). This M.S. is, he says, with great reason asserted to have been written in Italy above eleven hundred years ago."

The horizontal ⊢ which Dr. Jamieson took to be a contraction for VM, is found in Welsh Inscriptions of the 7th Century.

This is the only Latin Inscription yet found in the Island.

ROMAN ALTAR.

THERE is at Castle Rushen a Roman Altar which, however, was brought over from Cumberland between 1726 and 1731, as was clearly shown some years ago by Rev. T. Talbot in a letter to the *Manx Sun*.

It measures 3ft. 6in. high by 1ft. 4in. broad, and $11\frac{1}{2}$in. thick; and has the following Inscription on a panel $21\frac{1}{4}$in. long by 13in. broad:—

```
  I O V I . A V G.
  M.C E N S O R I V S.
  M·FLI·VOLTINIA·
    ]RNELIANVS· LEG.
    ]ETENSI[S]PRAE
    ]TVS· COH·TU
      ]EX.PROVINCIA
  N A R B O N   D O M O
  N E M A V S[   ]L.M.
```

Which Cumming, Fig. 50, expands—*Jovi Augusto Marcus Censorius Marci filius Voltinia (e tribu) Cornelianus legionis Tretensis præfectus cohortis Tungrensis ex provincia Narbonensi domo Nemaus. Votum solvit libens merito.*

BLF S N H D T C Q M G NG ST R   A O U E I

Fig. 7.

OGHAM ALPHABET ON MAL LUMKUN CROSS, MICHAEL.

OGHAM INSCRIPTIONS.

THIS is not the place to enter into a dissertation on the origin of the peculiar characters known as Oghams. Dr. Taylor, in his work already quoted [Greeks and Goths, p. 108] derives them from Runes of a very early type. Pointing out that their geographical distribution raises a strong presumption in favour of their Scandinavian origin, he proceeds to argue from the characters and names of the symbols that they must have been so derived, and suggests a primitive order and development of the Oghams in accordance with this theory, concluding that they might have been obtained from the Tuatha De Danann, whom he is inclined to identify with the Jutes from Jutland, "whose settlement in Kent and the Isle of Wight is the earliest Teutonic migration into Britain which can be called historical." Dr. Grant, Prof. Rhys, Prof. Stephens, and others, have ascribed different origins; that most recently suggested is by Prof. G. F. Browne, namely, from "finger signs" [*Academy, xxxviii, p.* 343.]

Over 150 Inscriptions have been found in Ireland, chiefly in the counties of Kilkenny, Waterford, Cork, and Kerry; some in Scotland and the Isles, and a few in Wales.

The first discovery of Oghams in the Isle of Man was in 1874, by the Rev. F. B. Grant, then Curate of Rushen, who submitted a drawing of one of the Ballaqueeney

Inscriptions to Mr Kneale, of Douglas, by whom it was deciphered. It appears not to have been published, however, till 1886, when the Rev. E. B. Savage contributed an account of it to the *Manx Note Book.*

The writer in 1889 was so fortunate as to discover on the face of the Mal Lumkun Cross at Michael, below the sculpturing, a perfect, though very faintly scratched and much worn, Ogham Alphabet. It is in the usual form and order, the vowels being full length twigs across a stem line, not notches, as with our other Oghams, where the "stem lime" is formed by the corner of the stone, which appear to be older.

ARBORY.

(1) I. Within the Friary, a slab of clay slate, 4ft. 4·5in. by 12in. by 6½in. The Inscription reads from left to right, up the edge of the stone; the legible portion occupying a space of 1ft. 9in. Evidently some is worn away from the beginning, as there are traces of Oghams 18 to 24in. below, and the end has been cut off.

. . . . . CUNAMAGLI MA[Q] . .

. . [ ] *of Cunamaglus son* [*of N.N.*]

RHYS.

(Manx Note Book, April, 1887; Academy, xxxiv., June, 1886.)

CUNAMAGLI MA[QI] &c.

BROWNE.

(Academy, xxxviii. p. 343, Oct. 1890).—The same reading. In Plate of illustrations to Lectures, given as above, in Oghams.

(2) II. Within the Friary, a granite boulder, 17in. by 16in. by 8 to 6in. thick. Inscription round the edge, occupying a space of about 18in.

MAQLEOG

Mac Leog.

RHYS.

(Academy, xxxiv., June, 1886.)—MAQLEOG or MACLEOGU (modern "Clague").

BROWNE.

(Academy, xxxviii., p. 343.) The same. In Plate,
MAQLEOGU.

MICHAEL.

(3) I. On the back of the Mal Lumkun Cross (No. 73 in the foregoing Catalogue) between the two runic legends, a Scratch Ogham, almost impossible now to decipher.

SOUTHESK.

(Academy, xxxv, p. 359, Nov. 1887).—The Earl of Southesk describes this from a drawing and description by Mr J. M. Nicholson and Rev. E. B. Savage, as follows :—

MUUCOMALL AFI UA MULLGUC.

Mucomael, son (grandson ? or descendant ?) of O'Maelguc.

(4) II. On the face of the same cross, as though to preserve a knowledge of the characters, with a view to letting the last inscription be read, is a perfect Ogham Alphabet—B, L, F, S, N, H, D, T, C, Q, M, G, NG, ST, R, A, O, U, E, I. It is to the right, and a little below, the sculpturing, occupying a space of 9in. long, the Oghams from ¾in. to 1½in. long, on a stem line ; it reads from below upwards. (See Fig. 7.)

BROWNE.

In Academy xxxviii, p. 343 (Oct. 1890) gives a description of it.

RUSHEN.

(5) I. At Ballaqueeney, a small slate stone, now measuring about 1ft. 8¾in. by 5½in. square. Most unfortunately it has been shattered to pieces by exposure to the weather, but the characters, well cut and well preserved, are nearly all in existence. The Inscription commencing 5½in. from the bottom, reads up the right edge of the stem, and round the top.

BIFAI [ ] NAS M[A]QI MUCOI CUNAFA.

(The Stone) of Bifai [do]n son of Mucoi Conaf.

KNEALE.

(Manx Note Book, October, 1887, p. 163.

BIFAIDONAS MAQI MUCOI QUNAFA.

[*The Stone*] *of Bifaidon, the son of Mucoi Conaf.*

RHYS.

(Manx Note Book, October, 1886, p. 146.)

The stone described by Rev. E. B. Savage, who gives Prof. Rhys' reading :—

BIVAICUNAS MAQI MUCOI CUNAVA.

In the Manx Note Book, April, 1887, p. 64, he suggests "dd" for "c" in the first name.

(6) II. At Ballaqueeney, a slab of lower Silurian Sandstone, measuring 3ft. 7in. by 14½in. by 4in. The Inscription occupies 2ft. 11¼in., of which 13½in. is left blank, dividing the word MAQI. This must be, as suggested by Prof. Rhys, that the stone just there is capped by quartz of extremely hard texture.

DOVAIDONA MA (space) QI DROAT

(The Stone) of Dovaido, son of the Druid.

RHYS.

(Manx Note Book, October, 1886, p. 147.)

Described by Rev. E. B. Savage, who gives the following reading by Prof. Rhys, by whom it was examined in the summer of that year :—

DOVAIDONA MAQI.

(Academy, xxxviii, p. 134, August 16th, 1890; Yn Lioar Manninagh, No. 6, p. 179). Prof. Rhys having again very carefully examined the stone, gives the reading as follows :—

DOVAIDONA MAQI DROATA.

Dovaido, son of (the) Druid.

BROWNE.

In Plate of Illustrations gives the Oghams for

DOVAIDONA MAQI DROATA.

PRINTED BY CHARLES BERNARD HEYES, RAMSEY, ISLE OF MAN.

CPSIA information can be obtained at www.ICGtesting.com
Printed in the USA
LVOW111440010213

318270LV00006B/303/P